Introduction
Harmonizing Music and Technology

Welcome to a revolutionary journey through the world of music and artificial intelligence, where creativity meets cutting-edge technology. Synthesized Sounds: A New Era is my personal gateway to sharing how the fusion of tunes and tech is redefining the music industry.

Through this book, I draw from my academic journey in Electronics Engineering Servicing, Video Communication Engineering Servicing, and Business Management to present a detailed guide for aspiring professionals keen to explore the exciting field of AI music. As an MIS expert serving in the Office of DMF Keonjhar under the Government of Odisha, I aim to bridge the gap between technical expertise and real-world applications, offering practical insights into this transformative career path.

Here, I delve into how AI is revolutionizing music creation, production, and distribution. This book highlights essential skills—from programming and sound engineering to entrepreneurial strategies—that can help anyone thrive in the rapidly evolving world of AI-driven music.
Whether you are a tech enthusiast, a passionate musician, or an innovator eager to leave your mark, I believe this book will inspire you to embrace and explore the possibilities of Synthesized Sounds - A New Era.
Welcome to the future of music!

Deepak Kumar Mahanta
Kendujhar, Odisha

Synthesized Sounds - A New Era

Synthesized Sounds - A New Era

Know Your Author

DEEPAK KUMAR MAHANTA
Bainsuli, Kendujhar
Odisha
PIN-858032
INDIA

Deepak Kumar Mahanta, the author of Synthesized Sounds - A New Era with the subtitle Tunes and Tech - Building a Career in AI Music, is an accomplished professional with a unique blend of technical expertise and managerial acumen.

With a Diploma in Electronics Engineering Servicing (DEES) and a Diploma in Video Communication Engineering Servicing (DVCES) from the Indian Technical Education Society (ITES), Deepak has a strong foundation in electronics and video communication technologies. His pursuit of excellence led him to further enhance his skills by obtaining a Master in Business Administration (MBA) from the Matrix Institute of Business Management (MIBM) in Journalism Management

Currently working as an MIS Expert in the Office of DMF Keonjhar under the Government of Odisha, Deepak seamlessly integrates his technical knowledge with administrative expertise. His passion for technology, especially in the realm of AI-driven music production, has fueled his writing of this insightful guide.

Synthesized Sounds - A New Era

Index

Synthesized Sounds - A New Era

Synthesized Sounds - A New Era

Synthesized Sounds - A New Era

1- The Evolution of Music Technology

1.1 Overview of Music Technology from Analog to Digital

The journey of music technology is a fascinating evolution from analog roots to the digital revolution that defines the modern era. This section explores:

1.1.1 The Analog Era:
The birth of sound recording with Edison's phonograph.
Vinyl records, magnetic tape, and the rise of analog synthesis.
How analog devices laid the foundation for **modern music production.**

1.1.2 The Transition to Digital:
The advent of digital audio and its transformative impact.
Compact Discs (CDs) and the rise of MIDI (Musical Instrument Digital Interface).
Early digital synthesizers, drum machines, and sampling technologies.

1.1.3 The Digital Domination:
The emergence of DAWs (Digital Audio Workstations) like Pro Tools and Logic Pro.
How MP3 and streaming platforms revolutionized music distribution.
AI-powered tools and their role in reshaping music creation and production.

This overview underscores the dynamic interplay between technology and creativity, setting the stage for understanding AI's revolutionary role in today's music landscape.

Synthesized Sounds - A New Era

1.2 Key milestones in the development of music production tools

Music production has undergone a radical transformation over the decades, driven by technological advancements. From the invention of basic recording devices to the integration of artificial intelligence in music creation, the evolution of music production tools reflects humanity's innovative spirit and its deep connection with sound. Here are the key milestones that have shaped the modern landscape of music production:

1.2.1. The Phonograph (1877)

Invented by Thomas Edison, the phonograph marked the beginning of recorded music. It was the first device capable of capturing and reproducing sound, revolutionizing how music could be preserved and shared.

Synthesized Sounds - A New Era

1.2.2. The Tape Recorder (1930)

Magnetic tape recorders introduced multitrack recording, allowing artists to layer sounds and instruments. This innovation laid the foundation for modern studio production techniques.

1.2.3. Analog Synthesizers (1960)

The introduction of analog synthesizers, such as the Moog Synthesizer, brought entirely new sounds to music production. These instruments enabled artists to experiment with electronic tones and textures, giving rise to genres like electronic and synth-pop.

Synthesized Sounds - A New Era

1.2.4. MIDI Protocol (1983)

The invention of the Musical Instrument Digital Interface (MIDI) was a game-changer. It allowed different electronic instruments and computers to communicate seamlessly, enabling unprecedented control and precision in music production.

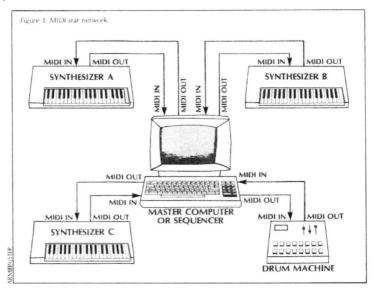

Figure 1. MIDI star network.

Synthesized Sounds - A New Era

1.2.5. Digital Audio Workstations (DAWs) (1990)

Software like Pro Tools and Cubase transformed music production by bringing powerful recording, editing, and mixing tools to personal computers. DAWs democratized music creation, making professional-grade production accessible to independent artists.

1.2.6. Auto-Tune (1997)

Introduced by Antares Audio Technologies, Auto-Tune became a defining tool in modern music. Beyond pitch correction, it introduced a unique vocal effect that has become a signature sound in many contemporary genres.

1.2.7. Virtual Instruments and Plugins (2000)

The development of virtual instruments and audio plugins expanded the sonic palette for producers. Tools like Native Instruments' Kontakt and Spectrasonics' Omnisphere offered realistic and experimental sounds, empowering artists to create without physical instruments.

1.2.8. AI-Powered Tools (2010-Present)

Artificial intelligence has opened new frontiers in music production. Platforms like Suno AI, AIVA, and OpenAI's MuseNet enable text-to-music generation, intelligent mastering, and even creative collaboration. AI tools are pushing the boundaries of what's possible in both composition and production.

1.2.9. Cloud-Based Collaboration and Distribution

Services like Soundtrap and Splice have introduced cloud-based collaboration, allowing artists from around the world to work together seamlessly. Simultaneously, platforms like DistroKid have simplified global distribution, helping independent artists reach listeners worldwide.

Synthesized Sounds - A New Era

1.2.10. Real-Time Music Separation and Remixing

Advancements in machine learning have led to tools like Vocal AI, which can separate vocals and instruments from a track in real time. This innovation is transforming remixing and post-production workflows.

Each of these milestones represents a step forward in music technology, empowering artists to express themselves in innovative ways. As we continue to explore AI-driven solutions and immersive technologies like virtual reality, the future of music production promises even greater possibilities. In this evolving landscape, understanding these milestones provides a solid foundation for building a career in AI-driven music creation.

1.3 The role of technology in shaping contemporary music genres

Music has always been a reflection of the technological advancements of its era. From the invention of the phonograph to the rise of digital audio workstations (DAWs) and artificial intelligence (AI), technology has continually shaped the way music is created, distributed, and consumed. In this chapter, we explore how technology has influenced the evolution of contemporary music genres, redefining artistic expression and broadening creative possibilities.

1.3.1. The Early Days of Music Technology

The journey began with mechanical instruments and analog recording devices. The phonograph allowed music to be recorded and played back, enabling composers to reach audiences beyond live performances. The invention of magnetic tape and multitrack recording in the mid-20th century further revolutionized music production, giving rise to new genres like rock and roll and later, electronic music.

1.3.2. Digital Revolution: Synthesizers and MIDI
The 1980s saw the advent of digital synthesizers and MIDI (Musical Instrument Digital Interface), which opened up new realms of sound design. Artists could now layer complex arrangements with precision, creating genres such as synth-pop, house, and techno. Iconic instruments like the Roland TR-808 drum machine became synonymous with the sound of an era, influencing hip-hop, pop, and dance music.

1.3.3. The Role of the Internet and Streaming Platforms
The rise of the internet and streaming platforms fundamentally changed how music was distributed and consumed. Platforms like Spotify, YouTube, and SoundCloud democratized music, allowing independent artists to reach global audiences. This shift enabled the emergence of niche genres such as lo-fi hip-hop, vaporwave, and bedroom pop, which thrived in the digital ecosystem.

1.3.4. Artificial Intelligence and Music Creation
AI has become a game-changer in contemporary music. Tools like Suno AI and OpenAI's Jukebox allow artists to generate compositions from text prompts or remix existing tracks with ease. AI algorithms can analyze trends, predict listener preferences, and even create entire songs, pushing boundaries in genres like experimental electronic and ambient music.

1.3.5. Hybrid Genres and Cross-Cultural Influences
Technology has also facilitated cross-cultural collaborations, giving rise to hybrid genres. Traditional folk music is now being blended with electronic beats, as seen in genres like

Synthesized Sounds - A New Era

EDM-folk fusion. AI tools enable artists to experiment with instrumentation and styles from different cultures, fostering innovation and global connection.

1.3.6. Shaping the Future of Music

The future of music will likely see even deeper integration of technology. Virtual reality (VR) concerts, AI-powered instruments, and blockchain-based royalty systems are already reshaping the industry. As technology evolves, so will the genres it inspires, continuing to blur the lines between human creativity and machine intelligence.

Technology has been the driving force behind the transformation of contemporary music genres. From analog devices to AI-powered platforms, each innovation has expanded the horizons of artistic expression. As we stand on the cusp of a new era, it is clear that technology will remain an integral part of music's evolution, inspiring creators to explore uncharted territories and redefine what is possible.

Synthesized Sounds - A New Era

2- Understanding AI and Its Music Applications

2.1 Explanation of Artificial Intelligence and Machine Learning Concepts

Artificial Intelligence (AI) and Machine Learning (ML) are transforming the way we create, experience, and distribute music. Understanding these concepts is crucial for anyone looking to thrive in the new era of synthesized sounds. This section breaks down these technologies and explains their relevance to music applications.

2.1.1 What is Artificial Intelligence (AI)?

AI refers to the simulation of human intelligence by machines. It involves programming computers to perform tasks that typically require human cognition, such as problem-solving, decision-making, and pattern recognition. In essence, AI enables machines to "think" and "learn" from data, making them capable of adapting to new situations and improving their performance over time.

Core Features of AI:

➤ **Automation:** AI automates repetitive and complex tasks.

➤ **Learning:** AI systems can analyze data, identify patterns, and make predictions.

➤ **Natural Language Processing (NLP):** AI can understand and generate human language, essential for music lyrics generation.

➤ **Creativity:** AI tools can compose original music, design album art, and even suggest chord progressions.

2.1.2 What is Machine Learning (ML)?

ML is a subset of AI that focuses on enabling machines to learn from data. Instead of being explicitly programmed for every task, ML models are trained using algorithms that allow them to improve as they process more data. This learning process is what makes ML particularly powerful for applications like music composition and sound generation.

Types of Machine Learning:

A.Supervised Learning:

Machines learn from labeled data, making it suitable for tasks like genre classification.

B.Unsupervised Learning:

Algorithms discover patterns in unlabeled data, ideal for creating unique musical styles.

C.Reinforcement Learning:

Machines learn through trial and error, perfect for interactive applications like live performances with AI-driven instruments.

2.1.3 Applications of AI and ML in Music

AI and ML have revolutionized the music industry, enabling both artists and producers to explore new creative horizons.

2.1.3.1. Music Composition and Generation

> ➢ AI tools like Suno AI and OpenAI's MuseNet can generate melodies, harmonies, and even complete tracks based on textual prompts or pre-defined styles. These systems use deep learning techniques to understand musical patterns and replicate them innovatively.

Synthesized Sounds - A New Era

2.1.3.2. Lyrics Writing
➢ Using NLP, platforms like ChatGPT and Gravitywrite can generate meaningful and poetic lyrics. These tools analyze existing lyrics and suggest original phrases or song structures.

2.1.3.3. Sound Design and Mixing
➢ AI-powered tools like Vocal AI can separate vocals from instrumentals, allowing producers to remix or refine their tracks effortlessly. Machine learning algorithms also aid in mastering tracks by optimizing sound quality.

2.1.3.4. Personalized Recommendations
➢ Streaming platforms like Spotify and YouTube Music utilize AI to analyze listener preferences and recommend songs. This personalization is powered by ML models trained on user behavior.

2.1.3.5. Real-Time Interactions
➢ AI is increasingly used in live performances, with algorithms adapting to the tempo and mood of human musicians. For example, AI-powered instruments can improvise alongside artists in real time.

2.1.4 How AI Learns Music?
AI learns music through vast datasets of compositions, lyrics, and audio. These datasets are fed into neural networks, which identify patterns such as chord progressions, rhythmic structures, and melodic styles. The more diverse the dataset, the more versatile the AI becomes in generating music.

Synthesized Sounds - A New Era

2.1.4.1 Steps in Training an AI Model for Music:
- ➤ **Data Collection:** Gathering music in various genres and styles.
- ➤ **Feature Extraction:** Analyzing key elements like pitch, tempo, and harmony.
- ➤ **Model Training:** Using algorithms to learn patterns and relationships in the data.
- ➤ **Evaluation:** Testing the model's ability to create coherent and appealing music.

2.1.4.2 Benefits of AI in Music Production
- ➤ **Enhanced Creativity:** AI acts as a collaborator, inspiring artists with new ideas.
- ➤ **Efficiency:** Automation speeds up tasks like editing and mastering.
- ➤ **Accessibility:** AI democratizes music creation, enabling anyone to produce professional-quality tracks.
- ➤ **Diversity:** Machine learning generates unique compositions that challenge traditional norms.

2.1.5 Challenges and Ethical Considerations

While AI offers immense potential, it also raises questions about originality and intellectual property. Who owns an AI-generated song? How do we balance human creativity with machine capabilities? Addressing these issues is crucial for the sustainable growth of AI in music.

Artificial Intelligence and Machine Learning are not just tools; they are transformative forces shaping the future of music. By understanding these technologies and their applications, musicians and producers can unlock unparalleled creative possibilities, marking the dawn of a new era in music production.

Synthesized Sounds - A New Era

2.2 Current AI Technologies Used in Music Composition and Production

2.2.1. AI-Powered Lyrics Writing
  - ➢ **Platforms:**OpenAI (ChatGPT), Gravitywrite
  - ➢ **Applications:** Generating song lyrics based on user-provided themes, tones, or emotions.
  - ➢ **Benefits:** Saves time for creators, offers inspiration, and generates poetic content tailored to specific audiences.

2.2.2. Text-to-Music Generation
  - ➢ **Platforms:** Suno AI, MuseNet
  - ➢ **Applications:** Converting textual descriptions into musical pieces that align with the desired mood or genre.
  - ➢ **Benefits:** Allows creators to experiment with new sounds and compositions without requiring formal music training.

2.2.3. AI-Driven Music Separation and Enhancement
  - ➢ **Platforms:** Vocal AI, Spleeter
  - ➢ **Applications:** Isolating vocals from instrumental tracks, enhancing audio quality, and remixing.
  - ➢ **Benefits:** Enables precise editing and remixing of songs, opening new possibilities for creators and producers.

2.2.4. Music Arrangement and Production
  - ➢ **Platforms:** AIVA (Artificial Intelligence Virtual Artist), Amper Music

- **Applications:** Composing original music scores, arranging melodies, and creating soundtracks for various projects.
- **Benefits:** Speeds up the production process and provides creators with fully arranged, ready-to-use compositions.

2.2.5. Sound Design and Effects
- **Platforms:** LANDR, Boomy
- **Applications:** Creating custom sounds, generating sound effects, and mastering tracks.
- **Benefits:** Enhances the overall sound profile and professionalizes the final output.

2.2.6. Real-Time Music Collaboration Tools
- **Platforms:** Soundtrap, Endlesss
- **Applications:** Facilitating collaboration between artists, producers, and AI systems in real-time.
- **Benefits:** Encourages creativity by enabling seamless interactions and live changes during the creative process.

2.2.7. AI-Powered Editing and Mixing
- **Platforms:** Kapwing AI, Adobe Audition AI
- **Applications:** Automating complex editing tasks, syncing tracks, and enhancing audio quality.
- **Benefits:** Reduces manual work and speeds up post-production processes.

2.2.8. Visual Enhancements for Music
- **Platforms:** OpenAI DALL-E, Canva AI
- **Applications:** Generating album covers, promotional materials, and video visuals.

Synthesized Sounds - A New Era

➢ **Benefits:** Complements music projects with visually appealing designs that align with the artist's branding.

2.2.9. Music Recommendation and Personalization
➢ **Platforms:** Spotify AI, Pandora's Music Genome Project
➢ **Applications:** Recommending music based on user preferences and behavior.
➢ **Benefits:** Enhances listener experience and helps artists reach target audiences more effectively.

2.2.10. AI in Live Performances
➢ **Platforms:** Wave AI, AI-based MIDI Controllers
➢ **Applications:** Enhancing live performances with real-time generative music and effects.
➢ **Benefits:** Adds dynamic elements to live shows and allows performers to interact with AI-driven soundscapes.

2.2.11. AI-Powered Distribution and Marketing
➢ **Platforms:** DistroKid, AI in YouTube Music Analytics
➢ **Applications:** Automating the distribution process, optimizing marketing strategies, and analyzing audience feedback.
➢ **Benefits:** Ensures efficient distribution and maximizes the reach of AI-generated music.

By leveraging these technologies, creators are not only able to produce high-quality music efficiently but also explore new realms of sound and creativity. The integration of AI tools into music composition and production is shaping the industry's future, offering endless possibilities for aspiring and professional artists alike.

Synthesized Sounds - A New Era

2.3 Case studies of Successful AI music projects

The advent of Artificial Intelligence (AI) in music has led to groundbreaking projects that redefine creativity and artistry. From generating music to producing albums, AI has been instrumental in empowering musicians and reshaping the music industry. This section highlights key case studies of successful AI music ventures, including the trailblazing work of India's LoudWave Studio.

2.3.1. LoudWave Studio, India

LoudWave Studio has set a benchmark in the Indian AI music space. By integrating AI tools such as Gravitywrite, Suno AI, Vocal AI, Kapwing AI, and OpenAI's DALL·E, LoudWave Studio has created an extensive repertoire of music spanning diverse genres.

Key Achievements:

- ***Bollywood Restore Songs:*** *LoudWave Studio's AI-generated Bollywood Restore Songs.*
- ***Patriotic Anthems:*** *By leveraging AI tools, LoudWave Studio produced inspirational songs like "Ae Mere watan ke logon" which celebrate Indian pride and patriotism.*
- ***AI Integration:*** *Every aspect of music creation—from lyrics writing to cover art design—is seamlessly executed with AI tools, ensuring high-quality production.*

Synthesized Sounds - A New Era

2.3.2. AIVA (Artificial Intelligence Virtual Artist)

AIVA, one of the pioneers in AI music composition, specializes in creating orchestral soundtracks. AIVA's compositions are used in films, video games, and advertisements. Its ability to generate classical music has earned it recognition from institutions like SACEM (Society of Authors, Composers, and Publishers of Music).

Key Achievements:
- **Film Scores:** AIVA's soundtracks have been featured in several indie films, showcasing its versatility.
- **AI Learning:** AIVA continuously improves its compositions by analyzing the works of classical composers like Beethoven and Mozart.

2.3.3. Endlesss

Endlesss is a collaborative music-making platform powered by AI. It allows users to create music in real-time and share it with a global community. By integrating AI tools, Endlesss simplifies the music creation process for beginners and professionals alike.

Key Achievements:
- **Real-Time Collaboration:** Musicians worldwide can create and edit music together instantly.
- **Ease of Use:** Endlesss' user-friendly interface makes it accessible to everyone, regardless of technical expertise.

2.3.4. OpenAI's Jukebox

OpenAI's Jukebox is a neural network capable of generating music in various genres and styles. From pop to jazz, Jukebox demonstrates the potential of AI to emulate human-like creativity.

Synthesized Sounds - A New Era

Key Achievements:
- *Genre Versatility:* Jukebox can replicate the styles of specific artists, offering unprecedented customization for creators.
- *Experimental Projects:* Several independent artists have used Jukebox to explore new musical directions.

2.3.5. Amper Music

Amper Music is an AI music composition tool designed for content creators. It enables users to quickly generate royalty-free music tailored to their projects.

Key Achievements:
- **Scalable Solutions:** Amper's platform is widely used for creating background music for videos, podcasts, and advertisements.
- **Customizable Tracks:** Users can adjust parameters like tempo, mood, and genre to align with their creative vision.

Synthesized Sounds - A New Era

3- AI Music Landscape

3.1 Exploration of the different players in the AI music industry

The AI music industry is evolving rapidly, with numerous players contributing to this transformative landscape. From startups pioneering innovative tools to tech giants leveraging AI for music creation, the ecosystem is diverse and dynamic. This chapter explores the major players, their unique offerings, and how they are shaping the future of music.

3.1.1. Tech Giants Leading the Charge

a) Google AI:

Google has been at the forefront of AI music research through initiatives like Magenta, an open-source research project exploring machine learning in art and music. Magenta has introduced tools like NSynth (Neural Synthesizer), which uses deep learning to create entirely new sounds, pushing the boundaries of traditional music composition.

b) OpenAI:

OpenAI's advancements, such as MuseNet, a deep neural network capable of generating compositions across multiple genres and styles, showcase the potential of AI in creating music with high complexity. Their contributions highlight how AI can blend classical and contemporary influences seamlessly.

c) Apple and Amazon:

Apple's integration of AI into platforms like GarageBand and Amazon's AI-driven personalized playlists on Amazon Music demonstrate how these companies are enhancing user experiences with intelligent music solutions.

3.1.2. Startups Pioneering Innovation

a) AIVA (Artificial Intelligence Virtual Artist):

AIVA specializes in composing emotional soundtracks for films, games, and advertising. Its ability to mimic human emotion in compositions has made it a favorite among creators looking for affordable and customizable music.

b) Amper Music:

Amper Music enables users to create royalty-free music quickly by selecting moods, instruments, and genres. Its intuitive platform empowers even non-musicians to generate professional-quality tracks.

c) Suno AI:

Suno AI's innovative approach to text-to-music generation bridges the gap between creative ideas and musical output, making it a valuable tool for independent artists and content creators.

3.1.3. Collaborative Platforms and Tools

a) Soundtrap by Spotify:

Soundtrap combines traditional music production tools with AI-powered features, allowing collaboration among musicians across the globe. Its integration with Spotify provides seamless sharing and distribution.

Synthesized Sounds - A New Era

b) BandLab:
BandLab's AI-driven tools, such as SongStarter, help artists overcome creative blocks by generating musical ideas based on user input.

c) Endel:
Endel creates personalized sound environments using AI, focusing on wellness and productivity. Its unique approach highlights the versatility of AI in music beyond traditional entertainment.

3.1.4. Academic and Research Institutions
a) MIT Media Lab
MIT's Media Lab explores the intersection of AI and music through projects that focus on algorithmic composition, interactive performances, and AI-assisted musical instruments.

b) Stanford CCRMA (Center for Computer Research in Music and Acoustics)
Stanford's CCRMA integrates AI into music research, emphasizing real-time interaction between human performers and AI systems.

c) Berklee College of Music
Berklee's adoption of AI tools in its curriculum reflects the growing importance of AI in music education, preparing students for future opportunities in the industry.

3.1.5. Ethical and Regulatory Players
a) Creative Commons
Organizations like Creative Commons play a vital role in addressing licensing and copyright issues in AI-generated music, ensuring fair usage and distribution.

b) Advocacy Groups
Groups advocating for ethical AI, such as AI Now Institute, emphasize transparency, accountability, and inclusivity in the AI music industry.

The AI music landscape is a mosaic of diverse players—each contributing uniquely to the field. By understanding the roles and innovations of these entities, aspiring musicians, producers, and technologists can identify opportunities to collaborate, create, and carve a niche in this exciting domain. This interconnected ecosystem promises to redefine how music is created, consumed, and appreciated in the digital age.

3.2 Overview of Software and Platforms Specializing in AI-Generated Music

The rise of artificial intelligence has ushered in a transformative era in the music industry, redefining how music is composed, produced, and distributed. This chapter delves into the tools and platforms that have emerged as frontrunners in AI-generated music, offering creators unprecedented opportunities to innovate and thrive. Below is an overview of some of the most notable software and platforms, categorized by their specialization and utility.

Synthesized Sounds - A New Era

3.2.1. AI for Lyrics Writing

- ➢ **ChatGPT (OpenAI):** Renowned for its natural language processing capabilities, this tool assists creators in crafting meaningful and poetic lyrics. Its ability to understand themes, moods, and rhymes makes it a go-to resource for songwriters.
- ➢ **Gravitywrite:** Focused on generating lyrics tailored to specific genres and themes, Gravitawrite provides targeted suggestions for building lyrical narratives.

3.2.2. Text-to-Music Generation

- ➢ **Suno AI:** Pioneering in transforming textual inputs into musical outputs, Suno AI enables users to generate complete melodies and instrumentals from simple descriptions. Its library includes diverse genres, making it versatile for various musical styles.
- ➢ **AIVA (Artificial Intelligence Virtual Artist):** AIVA specializes in composing soundtracks and symphonies, widely used for films, video games, and other media. Its advanced algorithms ensure compositions have a professional and emotional touch.

3.2.3. Music Separation and Processing

- ➢ **Vocal AI:** Designed to isolate vocals from instrumentals, Vocal AI is essential for remixing, re-arranging, or enhancing tracks. It provides precision in separating audio elements, enabling seamless reusability.
- ➢ **Spleeter:** An open-source tool developed by Deezer, Spleeter allows users to separate stems of audio files, offering flexibility for DJs and producers.

Synthesized Sounds - A New Era

3.2.4. Track Editing and Enhancement

- **Kapwing AI:** An intuitive tool for editing audio and video, Kapwing AI provides features like trimming, layering, and synchronizing tracks. Its simplicity caters to both beginners and professionals.
- **Audacity:** A widely popular, open-source audio editing platform that complements AI tools by allowing advanced editing and mastering of AI-generated content.

3.2.5. Visual Design for Music

- **DALL·E (OpenAI):** This AI tool is excellent for creating unique and compelling cover art for music releases. Its ability to generate high-quality, customized visuals adds a professional touch to any project.
- **Canva:** While not exclusively AI-driven, Canva's user-friendly interface and templates are enhanced with AI design suggestions, making it invaluable for branding and promotions.

3.2.6. Music Distribution and Promotion

- **DistroKid:** A leading platform for music distribution, DistroKid simplifies the process of uploading and monetizing tracks on major streaming platforms like Spotify, Apple Music, and YouTube.
- **TuneCore:** Similar to DistroKid, TuneCore offers extensive distribution services, analytics, and revenue tracking, empowering artists to manage their music careers effectively.

Emerging AI Innovations

The AI music landscape continues to evolve, with innovations focusing on real-time music generation, interactive compositions, and tools that bridge the gap between AI and human creativity. Platforms like Google's Magenta and OpenAI's MuseNet demonstrate how AI can collaborate with artists to co-create stunning works.

AI tools offer unmatched accessibility and efficiency, democratizing music creation for artists at all levels.

The synergy between human creativity and AI's computational power fosters unique and groundbreaking compositions.

Understanding the capabilities of each tool is crucial for leveraging their full potential in building a successful career in AI music.

The proliferation of these platforms signifies a new era where technology and artistry converge, empowering creators to push the boundaries of music. The next sections will delve deeper into practical applications and strategies for integrating these tools into your workflow.

3.3 The Impact of Music Streaming Services on AI Integration

The advent of music streaming services has revolutionized the way we consume, discover, and interact with music. Platforms like Spotify, Apple Music, and YouTube Music have not only democratized access to global music libraries but have also set the stage for the seamless integration of artificial intelligence (AI) into the music industry. This integration is redefining how music is created, curated, and consumed, marking a pivotal moment in the evolution of the industry.

3.3.1 Enhanced Personalization and Discovery

Music streaming platforms leverage AI to offer highly personalized user experiences. Algorithms analyze user preferences, listening habits, and contextual data to recommend tracks, playlists, and artists. This level of personalization has become a cornerstone of modern streaming services, with AI acting as a bridge between listeners and creators. For artists using AI tools to compose or produce music, this creates opportunities to reach niche audiences who are likely to appreciate their unique, algorithmically-enhanced creations.

3.3.2 AI-Driven Music Creation

Streaming services have also influenced the rise of AI in music creation. The demand for diverse and constant content has led artists and producers to adopt AI tools to compose tracks more efficiently. Platforms like Suno AI and OpenAI's music models allow creators to generate instrumental compositions, experiment with genres, or even develop fully produced tracks in record time. Streaming services, in turn, provide an ideal distribution channel for these AI-generated works, exposing them to millions of potential listeners worldwide.

3.3.3 Content Analysis and Curation

AI-powered content analysis tools play a critical role in categorizing and curating music for streaming platforms. From analyzing tempo and mood to identifying instruments and genres, AI enables platforms to maintain extensive, well-organized libraries. This analytical capability is invaluable for artists utilizing AI in music production, as it ensures their work is accurately categorized and easily discoverable by the right audiences.

3.3.4 The Rise of Independent Artists

Music streaming services have empowered independent artists, many of whom are now leveraging AI to compete with major labels. AI tools provide indie creators with access to professional-grade music production capabilities at a fraction of the cost. Coupled with the distribution power of streaming platforms, AI allows these artists to produce and release music that can rival mainstream productions in quality and reach.

3.3.5 Monetization Opportunities

AI integration has also opened new monetization avenues in music streaming. Streaming platforms' AI algorithms help creators maximize revenue by optimizing track placements, playlist inclusions, and listener engagement. Moreover, AI-generated music is increasingly being licensed for commercial use, including advertisements, video games, and film scores, providing creators with additional income streams.

3.3.6 Challenges and Ethical Considerations

While the impact of AI integration in music streaming is largely positive, it also raises challenges. Issues such as copyright disputes, the authenticity of AI-generated music, and the potential displacement of human musicians are critical topics that the industry must address. Streaming services must balance innovation with ethical considerations to foster a sustainable ecosystem for both human and AI-driven artistry.

3.3.7 Future Implications

As AI continues to evolve, its integration with music streaming services is poised to deepen. The next generation of streaming platforms may feature AI-generated virtual artists, real-time adaptive playlists, and even AI-guided collaborations between human artists. These advancements will further blur the lines between technology and artistry, offering unprecedented opportunities for creators and audiences alike.

Music streaming services have been instrumental in accelerating the integration of AI into the music industry. By providing a global platform for AI-generated content, enhancing discovery and personalization, and enabling new monetization models, these services are shaping a new era of music creation and consumption. For aspiring artists and music professionals, understanding this landscape is crucial to building a successful career in the evolving world of AI music.

Synthesized Sounds - A New Era

4- Building Your Creative Foundation

4.1 The Importance of Fundamental Music Theory and Composition Skills

In the rapidly evolving world of music production, especially in the era of AI-assisted tools, it's tempting to rely entirely on technology for creating sounds and compositions. While AI can generate melodies, harmonies, and entire arrangements, the creative decisions that shape truly unique music still rest on the artist's understanding of musical fundamentals. This is why building a solid foundation in music theory and composition remains vital, even in an age dominated by synthesized sounds.

4.1.1 Understanding the Core of Music
Music theory provides a framework for understanding how music works. It explains the relationships between notes, the structure of scales, and the dynamics of rhythm and harmony. By mastering these concepts, musicians and producers gain the ability to:
- **Compose with Intention:** Knowing why certain chords evoke specific emotions or how rhythm affects the flow of a piece empowers you to craft compositions that resonate with your audience.
- **Analyze and Adapt:** Music theory allows you to dissect existing works and apply their principles to your own creations, fostering innovation without losing coherence.

- **Communicate Effectively:** Whether collaborating with other artists or fine-tuning AI-generated outputs, a shared understanding of musical terminology and structure streamlines the creative process.

4.1.2 The Role of Composition Skills

Composition goes hand in hand with music theory, focusing on the art of creating new music. Strong composition skills ensure that you can bring your ideas to life, regardless of the tools you use. This becomes especially crucial in AI music production, where raw outputs often require human refinement to reach their full potential.

Through composition training, you develop:
- ➢ **Creative Problem-Solving:** Adapting and refining musical ideas becomes easier when you understand how to resolve harmonic and rhythmic challenges.
- ➢ **Versatility Across Styles:** Whether you're crafting ambient soundscapes or high-energy pop tracks, composition skills allow you to tailor your music to suit different genres and moods.
- ➢ **A Personal Signature:** In a world where AI often generates similar-sounding outputs, your unique compositional voice sets you apart.

4.1.3 Bridging Tradition and Innovation

As AI tools increasingly democratize music production, the importance of human creativity and expertise cannot be overstated. Fundamental music theory and composition skills provide a bridge between traditional musical practices and modern technological possibilities. With these skills, you can guide AI to enhance, rather than replace, your creative vision.

Synthesized Sounds - A New Era

By prioritizing these fundamentals, you build a robust creative foundation—one that supports not just individual pieces but an entire career in music, powered by both tunes and tech.

4.2 Techniques for developing a personal musical style

Developing a personal musical style is an integral part of standing out in the rapidly evolving field of AI-driven music creation. In this era, where synthesizers, algorithms, and creativity merge, defining your unique sound is both an art and a strategy. Here are practical techniques to help you craft your distinct musical voice:

4.2.1. Understand Your Influences
Every artist begins with inspiration. Reflect on the music that moves you and analyze why it resonates. Is it the rhythmic complexity, melodic simplicity, or emotional depth? Study these elements and allow them to shape your foundation without becoming mere imitations.

4.2.2. Experiment with Tools and Technology
AI and digital synthesizers offer an extensive palette of sounds. Dive deep into your tools, whether it's a DAW (Digital Audio Workstation) like Ableton Live or AI platforms like AIVA or Amper Music. Experiment with combinations of effects, presets, and generated sounds to uncover textures that feel uniquely yours.

4.2.3. Blend Genres and Cultures
Innovation often lies at the intersection of the unexpected. Mix genres or incorporate musical elements from diverse cultures. For example, layering traditional instruments over AI-generated beats can result in a rich, novel sound.

Synthesized Sounds - A New Era

4.2.4. Harness Improvisation and Spontaneity

Allow yourself to deviate from planned structures. Use real-time improvisation with synthesizers or live jam sessions with AI tools to capture spontaneous moments of creativity. These unpolished ideas can later evolve into signature elements of your style.

4.2.5. Focus on Emotion and Narrative

Your music should tell a story or evoke emotions that listeners connect with. Whether through lyrical themes, harmonic progressions, or soundscapes, align your creations with your personal experiences and vision. Authenticity often becomes the hallmark of a unique style.

4.2.6. Develop a Signature Sound Palette

Identify key sonic elements that will recur in your works, like a specific synth patch, drum pattern, or chord voicing. Consistency in certain aspects of your sound helps listeners associate your music with your identity.

4.2.7. Iterate and Refine

Revisit your older tracks periodically. Evaluate how your style is evolving and identify patterns or traits that feel distinctive. Use this feedback loop to refine and focus your creative process.

4.2.8. Collaborate with Other Creatives

Partnering with other musicians, producers, or visual artists exposes you to new perspectives. Collaborative projects can help you see your work from different angles, often unlocking new stylistic possibilities.

4.2.9. Leverage AI to Enhance, Not Replace, Creativity

AI should serve as an extension of your imagination, not a substitute for it. Use AI tools to generate ideas, but infuse them with your own sensibilities. This balance ensures your music remains personal and human-centric, even in a tech-driven world.

4.2.10. Embrace Feedback and Growth

Share your music with trusted mentors, peers, or even AI-based feedback systems. Constructive criticism is invaluable in helping you fine-tune your style. Stay open to growth while staying true to your core artistic values.

By implementing these techniques, you'll not only develop a distinct personal style but also position yourself as a unique voice in the emerging landscape of AI-enhanced music. Your creative foundation is the cornerstone of a meaningful and impactful musical journey.

4.3 Resources for Learning Music Production and Songwriting

In the dynamic world of AI-driven music production, building a strong creative foundation is essential. Whether you're an aspiring songwriter or a producer eager to experiment with synthesized sounds, having the right resources at your fingertips can accelerate your journey. Here's a curated list of resources to help you master music production and songwriting:

4.3.1. Online Learning Platforms

a. Skillshare & MasterClass

- ➤ **Skillshare**: Offers beginner-friendly tutorials on digital audio workstations (DAWs), sound design, and mixing. Look for courses by industry professionals who focus on specific genres or tools.
- ➤ **MasterClass**: Features lessons from legends like Hans Zimmer (film scoring) and Deadmau5 (electronic music production).

b. Coursera & edX

- ➤ Coursera provides university-led courses, such as Berklee College of Music's "Introduction to Music Production."
- ➤ edX offers programs that cover both theory and production, often with certifications.

4.3.2. DAW-Specific Tutorials

Every DAW (Digital Audio Workstation) has a unique workflow. Choose one that suits your style and master it using these resources:

- ➤ **Logic Pro X**: Check out Apple's official tutorials and communities like Logic Pro Help.
- ➤ **Ableton Live**: Dive into their learning hub (learn.ableton.com) and explore YouTube channels like Loopop for advanced techniques.
- ➤ **FL Studio**: Image-Line's website offers detailed guides, while creators like Busy Works Beats break down complex ideas for beginners.

4.3.3. Books for Music Production and Songwriting

- ➤ **"The Mixing Engineer's Handbook"** by Bobby Owsinski: A goldmine for understanding mixing techniques.

Synthesized Sounds - A New Era

- ➤ **"Writing Better Lyrics"** by Pat Pattison: Perfect for songwriters looking to refine their lyrical creativity.
- ➤ **"Dance Music Manual"** by Rick Snoman: A comprehensive guide for electronic music producers.

4.3.4. Communities and Forums

- ➤ **Reddit**: Subreddits like r/WeAreTheMusicMakers and r/EDMProduction provide tips, feedback, and peer support.
- ➤ **Gearspace (formerly Gearslutz)**: A forum for discussing production gear and techniques.

4.3.5. AI-Powered Tools and Tutorials

Given the theme of this book, leveraging AI tools is crucial for staying ahead:

- ➤ **LANDR**: Offers AI mastering services and a library of royalty-free loops.
- ➤ **Amper Music**: Learn how to create soundscapes with AI-assisted compositions.
- ➤ **Endlesss**: An app for collaborative AI-powered jam sessions.

4.3.6. Free Resources for Hands-On Practice

- ➤ **Splice**: Explore sample packs and presets to fuel your creativity.
- ➤ **YouTube Channels**: Check out *ADSR Music Production Tutorials* and *MusicTechHelpGuy* for free step-by-step lessons.
- ➤ **Kadenze**: Free and paid courses, including music theory and production techniques.

4.3.7. Collaborating with AI Music Platforms

Experimenting with tools that incorporate AI can be transformative:

Synthesized Sounds - A New Era

- ➤ **Magenta (by Google)**: Offers tools like NSynth for creating innovative sounds.
- ➤ **AIVA (Artificial Intelligence Virtual Artist)**: Assists in generating compositions based on your preferred style.

By combining these resources with consistent practice, you can build a solid foundation for exploring the limitless possibilities of music production and songwriting. As AI continues to revolutionize the music industry, staying informed and adaptive is the key to success.

Synthesized Sounds - A New Era

5- Tools of the Trade Software and Hardware

5.1 A guide to essential DAWs (Digital Audio Workstations) for AI music.

The rapid evolution of AI-driven music production has blurred the boundaries between creativity and technology. At the heart of this innovation are Digital Audio Workstations (DAWs), the essential software tools that musicians, producers, and AI enthusiasts rely on to bring their sonic visions to life. Coupled with the right hardware, these tools provide the foundation for crafting music in the era of synthesized sounds. This chapter explores the key DAWs and hardware setups that empower artists in the AI music space.

5.1.1 Essential DAWs for AI Music Creation

Digital Audio Workstations are more than recording studios on your computer—they are creative hubs for arranging, editing, and producing music. With AI integration becoming a major trend, here are the DAWs that stand out in this field.

5.1.1.1 Ableton Live

- ➢ **Why It's Great for AI Music:** Known for its intuitive interface and real-time music manipulation, Ableton Live is a favorite among electronic musicians and AI-based creators. Its Max for Live environment allows for custom AI plugins and machine learning tools, making it a playground for innovation.
- ➢ **Features to Explore:** AI-driven MIDI effects, real-time sampling, and compatibility with AI music tools like OpenAI's MuseNet.

Synthesized Sounds - A New Era

5.1.1.2 Logic Pro

➢ **Why It's Great for AI Music:** Apple's flagship DAW is celebrated for its powerful editing capabilities and seamless integration with AI-powered plugins. With its Smart Tempo and Flex Time features, Logic Pro adapts beautifully to dynamic AI-generated music flows.

➢ **Features to Explore:** AI-assisted composition tools and advanced automation features for fine-tuning AI-generated layers.

5.1.1.3 FL Studio (Fruity Loops)

➢ **Why It's Great for AI Music:** FL Studio is beloved for its user-friendly interface and robust MIDI editing tools. Paired with AI plugins, such as those using generative algorithms, it excels at creating intricate beats and patterns.

➢ **Features to Explore:** The Piano Roll, paired with AI-based beat generators, is a treasure trove for rhythmic experimentation.

5.1.1.4 Cubase

➢ **Why It's Great for AI Music:** A pioneer in MIDI sequencing, Cubase integrates seamlessly with AI tools for composing, arranging, and mixing. Its chord assistant feature can be supercharged with AI for innovative harmonic ideas.

➢ **Features to Explore:** Integrated AI features like automatic chord detection and VST compatibility with generative AI tools.

5.1.1.5 Bitwig Studio

➢ **Why It's Great for AI Music:** Bitwig Studio shines with its modular design and open API, ideal for AI music experiments. The Grid, Bitwig's modular sound design environment, enables creators to integrate AI-generated patches directly into their projects.

➢ **Features to Explore:** Open controller scripting and integration with machine learning tools like Magenta Studio.

5.1.2. Hardware That Complements Your DAW

While DAWs form the backbone of your music production setup, hardware plays a critical role in enhancing creativity and workflow. Here's what you need:

5.1.2.1 MIDI Controllers

➢ **What They Do:** MIDI controllers are essential for interfacing with your DAW, allowing you to perform and manipulate sounds in real-time. AI-based tools often benefit from tactile control for fine-tuning parameters.

➢ **Top Picks:**
- **Ableton Push 2:** Perfect for Ableton Live users, with pads that integrate seamlessly with AI-driven loops.
- **Arturia KeyLab:** Versatile for all DAWs, especially when using AI-powered plugins.

5.1.2.2 Audio Interfaces

➢ **What They Do:** An audio interface bridges your computer with microphones, instruments, and studio monitors, ensuring high-quality audio input and output.

Synthesized Sounds - A New Era

➤ **Top Picks:**
- **Focusrite Scarlett 2i2:** A budget-friendly yet professional choice for small studios.
- **Universal Audio Apollo Twin:** Ideal for producers who require advanced processing and AI-enhanced plugins.

5.1.2.3 Studio Monitors and Headphones

➤ **Why They're Important:** Accurate sound reproduction is crucial for refining AI-generated music. High-quality monitors and headphones allow you to hear subtle details and make informed production decisions.

➤ **Top Picks:**
- **KRK Rokit Series:** Known for its precise sound and bass response.
- **Beyerdynamic DT 770 PRO:** Industry-standard headphones for critical listening.

5.1.2.4 AI-Compatible Devices

➤ **What They Do:** Devices like Neural DSP Quad Cortex or AI-enhanced grooveboxes bring AI directly into hardware workflows, merging software intelligence with physical control.

➤ **Top Picks:**
- **Roli Seaboard:** A revolutionary expressive MIDI controller that pairs well with AI-assisted instruments.
- **Native Instruments Maschine+:** Combines hardware groovebox features with AI-based beat creation tools.

Synthesized Sounds - A New Era

5.1.2. 5 Emerging AI Tools and Plugins for DAWs

With the growing influence of AI, plugins and standalone software have become integral to modern DAWs. These tools automate, enhance, and inspire music creation:

> - **Magenta Studio:** A suite of generative AI plugins for Ableton Live.
> - **Amper Music:** AI-powered composition that integrates easily with most DAWs.
> - **LANDR:** AI mastering software that simplifies the finalization process.

The fusion of DAWs, hardware, and AI has unlocked a new realm of musical possibilities. For aspiring AI music creators, mastering these tools is the first step toward building a dynamic career in this futuristic industry. Choose the software and hardware that align with your creative vision, and embrace the boundless potential of AI to shape your sound.

5.2 Recommended Plugins and Virtual Instruments for Music Creation

In the evolving landscape of AI-driven music production, having the right tools can significantly elevate your creative output. Plugins and virtual instruments serve as the backbone of digital music creation, providing the textures, tones, and tools necessary to craft professional-grade compositions. Here are some highly recommended options that cater to beginners and seasoned producers alike:

5.2.1. Synthesizers

5.2.1.1 Serum by Xfer Records: Known for its intuitive interface and high-quality sound, Serum is a go-to wavetable

Synthesized Sounds - A New Era

synthesizer. Its versatility allows producers to craft anything from lush pads to gritty basslines.

5.2.1.2 Massive X by Native Instruments: This powerful synthesizer offers rich sound design capabilities and is ideal for creating cutting-edge electronic music.

5.2.1.3 Omnisphere by Spectrasonics: A hybrid instrument that combines hardware integration with an expansive sound library, making it perfect for cinematic and experimental compositions.

5.2.2. Drum Machines and Samplers
5.2.2.1 Battery 4 by Native Instruments: A robust drum sampler with a wide array of drum kits, perfect for creating intricate percussion tracks.

5.2.2.2 Superior Drummer 3 by Toontrack: Ideal for realistic acoustic drum tracks, offering detailed control over drum mic placement and tuning.

5.2.2.3 Kontakt by Native Instruments: A versatile sampler that supports an extensive range of sample libraries, from orchestral instruments to experimental textures.

5.2.3. Effects Plugins
5.2.3.1 FabFilter Pro-Q 3: A high-quality equalizer plugin with unmatched precision, perfect for shaping and balancing your mix.

5.2.3.2 ValhallaDSP Plugins: Revered for their lush reverbs and delays, Valhalla plugins like *Valhalla VintageVerb* are staples in the producer's toolkit.

Synthesized Sounds - A New Era

5.2.3.3 Soundtoys Bundle: A collection of creative effects, including delay, distortion, and modulation, to add character and depth to your tracks.

5.2.4. AI-Powered Tools

5.2.4.1 iZotope Ozone: A mastering suite that uses machine learning to analyze your mix and provide tailored recommendations.

5.2.4.2 LANDR: An AI-driven mastering tool and distribution platform that simplifies the post-production process.

5.2.4.3 Endlesss Studio: A collaborative platform that integrates real-time jamming with AI-powered loop generation.

5.2.5. Digital Audio Workstations (DAWs) with Integrated Plugins

While standalone plugins are essential, many DAWs come equipped with powerful built-in tools:

5.2.5.1 Ableton Live: Features a comprehensive suite of instruments and effects, with an intuitive workflow for electronic music.

5.2.5.2 Logic Pro X: Includes Alchemy, a robust synthesizer, alongside a range of professional-grade effects and loops.

5.2.5.3 FL Studio: Popular among beatmakers for its ease of use and built-in tools like Harmor and Sytrus.
- ★ **Tips for Choosing Plugins**
- ❖ **Define Your Style**: Select plugins that align with the genre you want to create.

Synthesized Sounds - A New Era

- ❖ **Invest in Quality Over Quantity**: A handful of versatile, high-quality plugins will serve you better than a cluttered collection.
- ❖ **Leverage Free Options**: Explore free plugins like Spitfire Audio's *LABS* or Vital for professional-grade sounds without breaking the bank.

- ★ **Stay Updated**: Regularly update your tools to access the latest features and maintain compatibility with your DAW.

By integrating these plugins and virtual instruments into your workflow, you'll have the foundation to create dynamic, professional, and innovative tracks. Whether you're crafting ambient soundscapes or dancefloor anthems, the right tools can unlock endless possibilities in the realm of AI-powered music production.

5.3 Overview of Hardware Options for Music Production

In the modern landscape of music production, the choice of hardware is pivotal to achieving professional-quality results. The right hardware not only enhances creativity but also streamlines workflows, allowing musicians and producers to focus on crafting their sound. In this section, we explore essential and advanced hardware options for music production, catering to both beginners and seasoned professionals.

5.3.1. Digital Audio Workstation Controllers
DAW controllers bridge the gap between the physical and digital realms, offering tactile control over your software. Popular options include MIDI keyboards with assignable

knobs and faders, such as the **Akai MPK** series or **Novation Launchkey**. These tools enhance precision in mixing, sequencing, and live performances.

5.3.2. Audio Interfaces

Audio interfaces are the backbone of any studio setup. They convert analog signals from instruments and microphones into digital signals that your computer can process. Brands like **Focusrite Scarlett**, **Universal Audio Apollo**, and **PreSonus** are renowned for their high-quality preamps and low-latency performance.

5.3.3. Studio Monitors and Headphones

Accurate sound monitoring is critical for mixing and mastering. Studio monitors like the **Yamaha HS Series** or **KRK Rokit** deliver flat frequency responses, ensuring true-to-source playback. Complement these with professional headphones, such as **Audio-Technica ATH-M50X** or **Beyerdynamic DT 770 Pro**, for detailed listening in environments where monitors aren't practical.

5.3.4. Synthesizers and Drum Machines

For those diving into electronic music or sound design, hardware synthesizers like the **Korg Minilogue** or **Moog Subsequent 37** provide hands-on control and rich sound textures. Drum machines, such as the **Roland TR-8S** or **Elektron Model:Samples**, allow producers to craft unique beats and rhythms with ease.

5.3.5. Microphones

High-quality microphones are indispensable for recording vocals and instruments. Condenser microphones like the **Rode NT1-A** or **Shure SM7B** are industry standards for capturing detailed and warm audio.

Synthesized Sounds - A New Era

5.3.6. External Effects and Preamps

Hardware effects units and preamps add analog warmth and unique character to recordings. Options like the **Universal Audio 6176 Channel Strip** or **Eventide H9** are favored for their versatility in shaping sound.

5.3.7. Modular Systems

For advanced producers, modular synthesizers offer unparalleled customization and sonic experimentation. Systems from **Make Noise** and **Doepfer** enable users to build unique soundscapes through patchable modules..

5.3.8. Computers and Peripherals

Your computer is the hub of your music production setup. Apple's **MacBook Pro** or custom-built PCs with robust CPUs and ample RAM are popular choices. Pair them with peripherals like external SSDs for fast storage and reliable backup solutions.

Choosing the right hardware depends on your production goals, genre preferences, and budget. Whether you are creating AI-driven compositions or traditional tracks, investing in quality equipment will set the foundation for a seamless and inspiring production process.

6- Collaborating with AI

6.1 Strategies for Integrating AI Tools into the Creative Process

In the ever-evolving world of music production, artificial intelligence has emerged as both a collaborator and a catalyst for innovation. By leveraging AI tools effectively, artists can amplify their creativity, streamline workflows, and uncover new sonic landscapes. This chapter explores practical strategies for integrating AI into your creative process, ensuring harmony between human artistry and machine intelligence.

6.1.1. Understand the Capabilities of AI Tools
Before diving in, familiarize yourself with the strengths and limitations of the AI tools you plan to use. Modern AI tools can:
  - ➤ Generate melodies, harmonies, and rhythms.
  - ➤ Analyze music trends and provide insights into popular styles.
  - ➤ Optimize audio mixing and mastering processes.
By understanding these capabilities, you can align the technology with your artistic goals.

6.1.2. Define Your Creative Objectives
AI tools are most effective when guided by a clear creative vision. Identify what you want to achieve with your music:
  - ➤ Are you seeking inspiration for new compositions?
  - ➤ Do you need help optimizing the technical aspects of production?
  - ➤ Are you exploring experimental genres or sounds?

Synthesized Sounds - A New Era

With defined objectives, you can direct AI tools to serve specific purposes rather than letting them dictate the creative flow.

6.1.3. Incorporate AI into Brainstorming Sessions
Use AI as a brainstorming partner to generate fresh ideas. Tools like AI-powered composition software can create unique riffs, chord progressions, or lyrical concepts. While the suggestions may not always align with your vision, they can serve as starting points to spark innovation.

6.1.4. Collaborate, Don't Delegate
Think of AI as a collaborator rather than a replacement for human input. For instance:
- Use AI to generate multiple melody options, then refine them using your musical intuition.
- Let AI assist in sound design by tweaking presets or generating entirely new textures, which you can further personalize.

This approach ensures the final product retains your unique artistic signature.

6.1.5. Streamline Repetitive Tasks
AI tools excel at automating repetitive processes, freeing you to focus on creative decisions. Leverage AI for:
- Audio editing, such as noise reduction or time alignment.
- Mixing tasks, like balancing levels or applying EQ.
- Generating MIDI patterns or loops that fit within your genre.

This can significantly reduce production time while maintaining professional quality.

6.1.6. Experiment with Genre-Blending

AI tools can analyze and synthesize sounds from various genres, enabling artists to explore uncharted musical territories. Use AI to merge styles, experiment with unconventional pairings, and create genre-defying music that challenges norms.

6.1.7. Analyze Audience Preferences

AI-driven analytics can provide insights into audience preferences, helping you tailor your music for greater impact. Tools can identify trending elements in popular songs, allowing you to incorporate similar themes while maintaining originality.

6.1.8. Embrace a Feedback Loop

Test and refine your work by creating an iterative feedback loop between you and the AI. For example:

> ➢ Generate a base composition with AI.
> ➢ Adjust and add human elements.
> ➢ Use AI again to refine technical details like mastering.

This cyclical approach ensures continuous improvement and collaboration.

6.1.9. Stay Open to Learning and Adapting

The integration of AI into music is still evolving. Stay informed about advancements, experiment with new tools, and adapt your workflow as the technology matures. Consider joining communities or forums to exchange ideas and learn from fellow artists.

6.1.10. Balance Technology and Emotion

While AI can enhance technical precision, the emotional core of music comes from the artist. Use AI to augment your creativity, but let your emotions and experiences shape the

Synthesized Sounds - A New Era

narrative. The best music resonates because it's deeply human, even when created with the help of machines.

Integrating AI into the creative process is not about replacing musicians; it's about empowering them. By combining the analytical precision of AI with the emotional depth of human artistry, you can redefine what's possible in music. Remember, the tools are only as powerful as the artist wielding them. Embrace AI as your ally in this new era of synthesized sounds.

6.2 Understanding AI as a Collaborator Rather Than a Replacement

As artificial intelligence continues to redefine the boundaries of creativity, the concept of AI as a collaborator rather than a replacement becomes increasingly critical—especially in the realm of music. In this evolving landscape, where technology meets artistry, the synergy between human creativity and AI's computational brilliance has the potential to unlock new dimensions of innovation.

6.2.1 Reframing the Narrative

AI is often perceived as a disruptor poised to replace human roles, but this perspective overlooks its most transformative potential: collaboration. Instead of viewing AI as a competitor, it can be embraced as a tool that augments and enhances human creativity. In the music industry, AI's role is not to overshadow composers, producers, or performers but to empower them by automating repetitive tasks, generating novel ideas, and expanding the scope of what is creatively possible.

Synthesized Sounds - A New Era

For instance, AI can assist in composing melodies, harmonizing tracks, or even mastering recordings. However, these tools require human guidance—much like an orchestra needs a conductor. The interplay of human intuition and AI's data-driven insights creates a partnership that yields results neither could achieve alone.

6.2.2 The Role of Human Intuition

While AI excels at processing large volumes of data and identifying patterns, it lacks the emotional depth and intuition that characterize human artistry. Music is more than just notes and rhythms; it is an expression of emotion, culture, and storytelling. Human creators bring context, emotion, and a unique perspective that AI cannot replicate. This is why the collaboration between AI and humans holds such promise—it combines the efficiency and scalability of AI with the heart and soul of human creativity.

6.2.3 Practical Applications in Music Creation

Consider the following scenarios where AI acts as a collaborator in music creation:

6.2.3.1 Idea Generation:

➢ AI tools like Amper Music and AIVA can generate musical ideas or suggest chord progressions, offering fresh inspiration for artists experiencing creative blocks.

6.2.3.2 Customization and Adaptation:

➢ AI can analyze trends and audience preferences to help artists tailor their music for specific demographics or platforms.

Synthesized Sounds - A New Era

6.2.3.3 Real-Time Performance Assistance:
> AI-powered instruments and software can adapt to live performances, adding layers of improvisation or effects in sync with the artist's actions.

6.2.3.4 Remixing and Repurposing:
> AI can analyze an artist's existing works and suggest remixes or adaptations for different genres, opening up new markets for their music.

6.2.4 Fostering a Mindset of Collaboration
To thrive in this AI-enhanced era of music, artists and professionals must adopt a collaborative mindset. This means learning to use AI tools effectively, understanding their limitations, and knowing when to rely on human intuition.

Education and training play a crucial role in this transition. Musicians, composers, and producers should familiarize themselves with the capabilities of AI tools while honing their own creative and emotional intelligence. By doing so, they can fully harness AI's potential without compromising their unique artistic vision.

6.2.5 The Human-AI Symphony
The collaboration between humans and AI is much like a symphony orchestra: each player contributes something essential, and the conductor orchestrates these contributions into a harmonious whole. In the same way, musicians and AI tools can work together to create something greater than the sum of their parts.

By viewing AI as a partner rather than a replacement, the music industry can embrace a future where technology amplifies human artistry. This collaboration promises not only to enhance the creative process but also to

Synthesized Sounds - A New Era

democratize music creation, making it accessible to a broader audience.

Together, humans and AI are composing the soundtrack of a new era-one that celebrates both technological innovation and the timeless essence of human creativity.

6.3 Balancing Human Creativity with Technological Assistance

In the ever-evolving world of music, the collaboration between human creativity and AI technology has unlocked unprecedented potential. Yet, the key to truly thriving in this space lies in striking the right balance between the two forces. While AI offers efficiency, precision, and boundless possibilities, it is the human touch that brings emotional depth and individuality to every composition.

AI tools can compose, arrange, and even generate original melodies at lightning speed, but these outputs are often devoid of the personal and cultural nuances that define human artistry. As a musician, it's important to view AI as a partner rather than a replacement. Leveraging AI as a tool to amplify your ideas—whether it's by enhancing production quality, experimenting with genres, or automating mundane tasks—frees up time and energy to focus on the aspects of music that resonate deeply with listeners.

However, the collaboration comes with challenges. Over-reliance on AI can dilute the authenticity of a track, making it feel mechanical or impersonal. To prevent this, musicians should actively engage in the creative process—fine-tuning melodies, adding layers of emotion, and ensuring that the final product reflects their vision and identity. Consider AI as the ultimate collaborator: a source of inspiration, a brainstorming partner, and an assistant that expands your creative boundaries. But the essence of the music, the story it tells, the feelings it evokes, and the connections it builds must come from you.

In this chapter, we will explore practical ways to integrate AI tools into your creative workflow while preserving the authenticity of your artistry. By striking this balance, you can create music that is not only cutting-edge but also deeply human, carving out a unique niche in the AI-driven music industry.

Synthesized Sounds - A New Era

7- The Ethics of AI in Music

7.1 Discussion on Copyright and Ownership of AI-Generated Music

7.1.1 Blurred Lines of Creativity
- ➤ Traditional copyright laws assign ownership to human creators. AI challenges this by generating music without direct human input.
- ➤ Ambiguity arises in determining who owns the rights: the developer, the user, or the AI itself.

7.1.2 Ownership of the Algorithm vs. the Output
- ➤ Developers argue that they own the rights due to their creation of the AI model.
- ➤ Users claim ownership if they provide prompts, training data, or creative direction.

7.1.3 Collaborative Creativity
- ➤ AI often acts as a tool for human artists, raising questions about whether the output is co-authored.
- ➤ Establishing shared ownership models may provide a fair resolution in such cases.

7.1.4 Legal Frameworks Lagging Behind
- ➤ Existing copyright laws were not designed with AI in mind, leading to gaps in addressing AI-generated works.
- ➤ Global inconsistencies in legal treatment further complicate the landscape.

7.1.5 Ethical Considerations in Attribution

➢ Lack of transparency in AI-generated music can obscure original human contributions.

➢ Ensuring proper attribution can help maintain ethical standards in the music industry.

7.1.6 Case Studies and Precedents

➢ Landmark cases have started shaping interpretations of AI ownership, but outcomes remain inconsistent.

➢ Examples include disputes over AI-composed tracks and their licensing.

7.1.7 Economic Implications

➢ Ownership debates affect revenue sharing and monetization models in the music industry.

➢ Resolving copyright issues is crucial for ensuring fair compensation for all stakeholders.

7.1.8 Future of AI Music Ownership

➢ Potential solutions include creating new legal categories for AI-generated content.

➢ Licensing agreements tailored to AI could clarify ownership and ensure equitable distribution.

7.1.9 Role of Policymakers and Industry Leaders

➢ Governments, industry bodies, and tech companies must collaborate to address ownership challenges.

➢ Developing global standards for AI-generated content can provide long-term clarity.

This discussion highlights the urgent need for innovative legal and ethical frameworks to navigate the complex intersection of AI, creativity, and ownership in the evolving music landscape.

7.2 Ethical Considerations in Using AI to Replicate Styles or Artists

One of the most contentious issues in the intersection of artificial intelligence and music creation is the replication of styles or the emulation of specific artists. While AI-powered tools have opened up incredible creative possibilities, they also raise profound ethical questions that must be addressed by creators, consumers, and the music industry alike.

7.2.1. Intellectual Property and Ownership

When AI replicates the style of a well-known artist, it often skirts the boundaries of intellectual property (IP) laws. While an artist's style may not be copyrighted, specific compositions and recordings are. This ambiguity raises the question: does the replication of an artist's distinct style constitute infringement, or is it simply creative inspiration? Striking a balance between innovation and respect for existing IP is crucial to prevent exploitation.

7.2.2. Authenticity and Artistic Identity

For many artists, their style is an integral part of their identity. When AI mimics an artist's approach, it can dilute the authenticity of their work and potentially erode their cultural or commercial value. This raises concerns about how such technologies might commoditize artistic expression, reducing it to a replicable formula.

7.2.3. Consent and Compensation

Should artists be compensated or consulted when their styles are used by AI? The lack of clear frameworks for consent and royalties creates potential for unethical practices. Some argue that artists should have the right to opt out of having their work used to train AI models, while others call for systems that ensure fair compensation.

7.2.4. Impact on Emerging Artists
AI's ability to emulate established artists could overshadow the efforts of new musicians trying to develop their own unique sound. If industry stakeholders prioritize AI-generated music mimicking popular styles, it may stifle innovation and diversity in the music landscape.

7.2.5. Cultural Appropriation and Misuse
AI replication risks crossing into cultural appropriation, where historically significant or culturally specific styles are used without understanding or respect for their origins. This can be particularly problematic when these styles are stripped of context and commodified for profit.

7.2.6. The Role of Transparency
Ethical AI usage requires transparency. Listeners should be informed when a piece of music is AI-generated or heavily influenced by an algorithm trained on specific artists or styles. Such disclosure ensures accountability and enables informed consumer choices.

This excerpt ties into the broader narrative of how musicians and industry professionals can ethically and sustainably build careers in the evolving landscape of AI music.

While AI replication of styles or artists holds immense potential to democratize music creation, it must be wielded responsibly. Establishing ethical guidelines, respecting intellectual and cultural boundaries, and ensuring equitable systems for consent and compensation are critical steps in navigating this complex terrain. The future of AI in music should not only celebrate technological progress but also uphold the values of creativity, respect, and fairness.

7.3 Industry Standards and Guidelines Regarding AI in Music Creation

The integration of artificial intelligence (AI) into music creation has sparked a transformative wave in the music industry, presenting both opportunities and challenges. As the boundaries between human creativity and machine capabilities blur, the importance of establishing clear industry standards and guidelines becomes paramount. These standards are essential not only for ensuring ethical practices but also for fostering trust, transparency, and collaboration among creators, developers, and audiences.

7.3.1. Transparency and Attribution:
A key standard emerging in the AI-music landscape is the need for transparency regarding the role AI plays in the creative process. Industry guidelines recommend that artists disclose whether AI has been used in composition, production, or performance. This transparency respects audience expectations and helps maintain the integrity of human contributions.

7.3.2. Intellectual Property Rights:
One of the most pressing concerns in AI-driven music creation is the ownership of intellectual property. Industry standards are evolving to address questions like: Who owns a song generated by AI? Should credit be attributed to the programmer, the artist who guided the AI, or both? Guidelines

are being shaped to ensure fair distribution of rights and royalties.

7.3.3. Avoiding Plagiarism and Data Bias:

AI systems trained on existing music libraries risk inadvertently replicating or plagiarizing copyrighted material. Standards emphasize the use of properly licensed datasets for training AI models. Additionally, developers are encouraged to address potential biases in AI training data to ensure diverse and inclusive musical outputs.

7.3.4. Ethical Use of AI Models:

Industry guidelines are also focusing on the ethical implications of using AI to replicate specific artists' styles, voices, or performances without consent. Such practices raise concerns about authenticity, copyright infringement, and potential misuse of an artist's brand.

7.3.5. Collaboration and Innovation Frameworks:

As AI becomes a collaborator rather than merely a tool, the industry is adopting frameworks that encourage cooperation between AI developers, musicians, and producers. These guidelines aim to strike a balance between technological innovation and artistic freedom, ensuring that AI enhances rather than diminishes human creativity.

7.3.6. Standardization for Fairness and Accessibility:

Efforts are underway to standardize AI tools and platforms, making them accessible to a wider range of musicians, including independent artists. This democratization ensures that the benefits of AI in music creation are not limited to a privileged few but are available across the industry.

Synthesized Sounds - A New Era

7.3.7. Global Policy Harmonization:

Given the global nature of music and technology, harmonizing AI-related policies across regions is critical. International bodies and industry associations are working towards creating universally accepted guidelines to address issues of copyright, ethics, and data usage.

The establishment of robust industry standards and guidelines is essential for navigating the complex ethical terrain of AI in music creation. These frameworks not only protect the rights of creators but also ensure that AI serves as a catalyst for innovation and inclusivity in the evolving world of music. By fostering responsible AI practices, the music industry can embrace a future where technology and artistry coexist harmoniously.

Synthesized Sounds - A New Era

8- Marketing Your AI-Enhanced Music

8.1 Identifying Your Target Audience and Niche Market

In the world of AI-enhanced music, identifying your target audience and niche market is crucial to your success. The fusion of tunes and tech offers endless possibilities, but to make your mark, you must focus on the people who will resonate most with your creations.

8.1.1 Understanding Your Audience

Begin by asking yourself: Who will connect with your music? Is it tech-savvy listeners intrigued by futuristic sounds? Traditional music lovers seeking a fresh twist? Or gamers and filmmakers looking for innovative soundscapes? Knowing your audience's demographics such as age, geographic location, and preferences will help tailor your marketing strategies effectively.

8.1.2 The Power of Niche Markets

AI-enhanced music thrives in niche markets. Instead of competing with mainstream artists, focus on specialized areas where your sound has unique value. For example, AI-generated ambient tracks can appeal to meditation enthusiasts, while dynamic, AI-driven beats might attract electronic dance music (EDM) fans. By defining your niche, you can cultivate a loyal audience that values your distinct sound.

8.1.3 Conducting Market Research

Leverage data-driven tools and platforms to gather insights about your potential listeners. Analyze streaming trends, social media interactions, and genre popularity to understand your audience's preferences. Online communities, forums, and feedback on platforms like SoundCloud or Spotify can also provide valuable input.

8.1.4 Embracing Feedback

Audience engagement is a two-way street. Encourage feedback and interaction to fine-tune your music. AI offers the flexibility to adapt and experiment quickly, allowing you to respond to evolving audience preferences while staying true to your creative vision.

8.1.5 Tailoring Your Message

Once your target audience and niche are defined, craft a compelling message that resonates with them. Highlight the unique aspects of your music—whether it's the innovative use of AI, emotionally evocative compositions, or immersive storytelling through sound.

By identifying your target audience and carving out your niche, you lay the foundation for a sustainable career in AI-enhanced music. This focused approach not only amplifies your reach but also ensures your music finds the right ears in a rapidly evolving industry.

8.2 Building an Online Presence through Social Media and Platforms

In today's digital age, having a strong online presence is essential for marketing AI-enhanced music. Social media platforms and other digital channels provide artists with unparalleled opportunities to showcase their work, connect with fans, and build a global audience.

Synthesized Sounds - A New Era

8.2.1 Why Social Media Matters for AI Musicians

Social media is more than just a promotional tool; it's a space where artists can engage directly with listeners and share their creative journey. For AI-driven musicians, these platforms provide an opportunity to educate audiences about the unique aspects of their work, like how AI contributes to their soundscapes and compositions. This storytelling not only creates intrigue but also establishes your brand as innovative and forward-thinking.

8.2.2 Selecting the Right Platforms

Different social media platforms cater to different audiences, so choosing the right ones is critical. For AI-enhanced music, platforms like Instagram, YouTube, and TikTok are excellent for showcasing visual and audio content. YouTube can host videos explaining your creative process, while Instagram and TikTok are ideal for sharing short clips, behind-the-scenes footage, and live performances. Platforms like Twitter and LinkedIn, on the other hand, are great for connecting with industry professionals, sharing thought leadership, and announcing collaborations or events.

★ Crafting Engaging Content

To attract and retain followers, consistency and creativity are key. Use the following strategies to make your content stand out:

- ➢ **Showcase the Unique:** Share content that highlights how AI contributes to your music, such as videos demonstrating AI in action or interactive polls asking fans for input on AI-generated tracks.
- ➢ **Behind-the-Scenes Stories:** Post snippets of your creative process, including challenges and breakthroughs. This humanizes your work and builds a connection with your audience.

Synthesized Sounds - A New Era

- ➤ **Educational Content:** Many people are curious about how AI is transforming music. Create posts, reels, or short videos explaining the basics of AI in music production or offering tutorials on AI music tools.
- ➤ **Engage Through Interaction:** Reply to comments, host Q&A sessions, and conduct live streams to foster a sense of community around your brand.

8.2.3 Collaborating with Influencers and Platforms

Collaborating with influencers in the music and tech space can amplify your reach. Find influencers whose audiences align with your genre and values, and explore partnerships that showcase your AI-enhanced music. Additionally, uploading your music to platforms like Spotify, SoundCloud, and Bandcamp ensures it's accessible to a global audience.

8.2.4 Analytics: Measuring Success

Use analytics tools to monitor your performance on social media platforms. These insights help you understand what type of content resonates most with your audience, allowing you to refine your strategy for maximum impact.

By leveraging social media and online platforms effectively, you can transform your AI-enhanced music from a niche interest into a global phenomenon, building both your brand and your fanbase in the process.

8.3 Effective Strategies for Promoting AI Music Projects

In the rapidly evolving landscape of AI music, effective promotion is essential for standing out in a crowded

marketplace. **Below are some key strategies to elevate your AI music projects and connect with audiences:**

8.3.1. Leverage Social Media and Content Platforms

➤ Utilize platforms like Instagram, TikTok, and YouTube to share snippets, behind-the-scenes creation processes, and live performances of your AI-generated music.

➤ Engage audiences with visually compelling posts that highlight the fusion of technology and art.

➤ Collaborate with influencers and creators who are passionate about AI and music to amplify your reach.

8.3.2. Educate and Engage Your Audience

➤ Use blogs, webinars, or podcasts to explain the unique aspects of your AI-driven music creation process.

➤ Highlight the role AI plays in enhancing creativity while emphasizing your human touch as a creator.

➤ Share success stories or case studies to build credibility.

8.3.3. Collaborate with Industry Players

➤ Partner with established artists, producers, or labels to co-create AI-enhanced tracks.

➤ Explore cross-industry collaborations with tech companies or digital art platforms for unique campaigns.

➤ Showcase your music in tech-forward spaces such as gaming, virtual reality, or metaverse environments.

8.3.4. Optimize Streaming and Distribution

➤ Strategically release your music on popular streaming platforms like Spotify, Apple Music, and Deezer.

➢ Create AI-curated playlists that feature your tracks alongside complementary genres or artists.
➢ Optimize metadata and descriptions for discoverability on these platforms.

8.3.5. Host Interactive Experiences
➢ Organize live streams or virtual events where audiences can interact with your AI tools and see them in action.
➢ Consider gamifying your music experiences, allowing fans to remix or co-create tracks using AI.
➢ Participate in music-tech festivals or events to showcase your work.

8.3.6. Utilize Data-Driven Marketing
➢ Analyze streaming and social media data to understand listener demographics and preferences.
➢ Use AI-driven marketing tools to personalize your promotional efforts, tailoring ads and content to specific audience segments.
➢ Continuously test and refine campaigns based on real-time feedback and performance metrics.

8.3.7. Embrace Storytelling
➢ Craft a compelling narrative around your music and technology journey.
➢ Share stories that highlight the challenges and breakthroughs in creating AI-enhanced music.
➢ Use storytelling to connect emotionally with your audience, making your brand more relatable.

By implementing these strategies, artists can not only promote their AI music projects effectively but also position themselves as pioneers in this exciting new era of synthesized sounds.

9- Monetizing Your Music Career

9.1 Overview of Revenue Streams in the Music Industry

The music industry is a dynamic ecosystem offering a variety of revenue streams that artists, producers, and creators can tap into to sustain and grow their careers. For musicians embracing the integration of AI and technology, understanding these revenue streams is crucial for effectively monetizing their craft. Below are the primary sources of income in the music business, particularly relevant to the AI-driven landscape:

9.1.1. Streaming and Digital Downloads
With platforms like Spotify, Apple Music, and Amazon Music dominating the market, streaming has become a cornerstone of music revenue. AI can enhance discoverability through personalized playlists and recommendations, allowing artists to reach a global audience. Additionally, offering digital downloads through platforms like Bandcamp or artist-specific websites can supplement income.

9.1.2. Performance and Touring
Live performances remain a significant income source. Artists can leverage technology to enhance live shows with AI-driven visuals, holographic displays, and immersive soundscapes, creating unique concert experiences that attract fans. Virtual concerts and live-streaming platforms also present opportunities for monetization, especially in the digital-first era.

9.1.3. Merchandising

Selling branded merchandise, such as apparel, posters, or exclusive items, is a tried-and-true way to generate revenue. AI tools can help design custom merchandise or analyze fan data to create products tailored to audience preferences.

9.1.4. Royalties

- ❖ **Mechanical Royalties**:
- ➢ Earned from song sales or digital downloads.
- ❖ **Performance Royalties**:
- ➢ Generated when music is played on radio, TV, or streaming services.
- ❖ **Sync Licensing**:
- ➢ Income from licensing music for films, video games, and advertisements. AI tools can facilitate sync placements by matching tracks with visual media.

9.1.5. Content Creation and Partnerships

Artists can generate revenue by collaborating with brands for campaigns, advertisements, or exclusive AI music creations. Sponsorships and partnerships are increasingly lucrative, especially for those with strong social media or digital presence.

9.1.6. Crowdfunding and Fan Support

Platforms like Patreon and Kickstarter allow artists to seek direct financial support from fans. AI can help artists engage supporters by offering personalized rewards, such as AI-generated tracks or exclusive virtual meet-and-greets.

9.1.7. AI Music Tools and Licensing

As the music industry integrates AI, musicians can monetize their skills by creating AI-generated compositions, soundscapes, or tools for other creators. Licensing

AI-generated music or providing creative services through online platforms can open new income streams.

9.1.8. Educational Content and Workshops

Sharing knowledge through online courses, webinars, or workshops is a growing avenue for income. AI-generated content can enhance teaching materials, while platforms like YouTube or Udemy offer global reach.

By diversifying income streams and leveraging the latest technology, musicians in this new AI-powered era can create sustainable careers while reaching audiences in innovative and exciting ways.

9.2 Exploring Licensing, Streaming, and Live Performance Opportunities

In the ever-evolving music industry, monetizing your craft has transcended traditional record sales and moved into a multifaceted ecosystem. For musicians, especially those leveraging AI-powered music creation, exploring licensing, streaming, and live performance opportunities is pivotal to building a sustainable career.

9.2.1 Licensing: Amplifying Reach Through Rights

Licensing music involves granting permission for others to use your compositions in various contexts, such as films, advertisements, video games, or TV shows. This avenue is particularly lucrative for AI-based music creators, as the adaptability of synthesized sounds suits diverse industries. Platforms like Songtradr and AudioJungle enable artists to monetize their tracks by connecting them with clients seeking specific moods or themes. By understanding copyright laws and ensuring proper registration of your works, you can secure long-term revenue streams while retaining ownership rights.

9.2.2 Streaming: The Digital Airwaves

Streaming platforms have revolutionized music consumption. Services like Spotify, Apple Music, and YouTube allow artists to distribute their tracks to global audiences at minimal upfront costs. AI musicians can leverage these platforms to showcase their unique, genre-blurring creations and engage with niche audiences. Optimizing your streaming profile with detailed metadata, regular uploads, and curated playlists ensures visibility in a competitive marketplace. Additionally, consider exploring platforms dedicated to AI and experimental music, as they often attract tech-savvy listeners intrigued by innovative sounds.

9.2.3 Live Performances: The Human Connection

While AI-generated music often thrives in digital realms, live performances provide an irreplaceable connection with audiences. Incorporating visual elements like interactive AI art or dynamic projections can elevate the live experience. Events such as tech-centric music festivals, gaming expos, and industry showcases offer ideal venues to demonstrate the creative potential of AI in real-time. Monetization opportunities range from ticket sales to merchandise and sponsorship deals with brands aligned with your futuristic soundscape.

By diversifying these revenue streams, artists can create a resilient music career in an increasingly tech-driven landscape. Licensing, streaming, and live performances, when approached strategically, allow AI musicians to transform their passion into a sustainable livelihood, reaching global audiences in ways traditional methods could never achieve.

Synthesized Sounds - A New Era

9.3 Selling Digital Products and Services Related to AI Music

In the digital age, the music industry is no longer confined to traditional methods of production and distribution. With advancements in artificial intelligence (AI), musicians now have the opportunity to explore innovative revenue streams by creating and selling AI-driven digital products and services. This is especially relevant for artists looking to monetize their skills while leveraging cutting-edge technology.

9.3.1. AI-Generated Music Tracks and Loops

AI music tools enable artists to create unique, royalty-free music tracks, loops, and samples that can be sold to producers, content creators, and filmmakers. These AI-assisted compositions provide an efficient way to cater to the growing demand for background music in podcasts, YouTube videos, advertisements, and more. Platforms like Splice and BeatStars serve as ideal marketplaces to showcase and sell your AI-generated sounds.

9.3.2. Personalized AI Music Tools

If you have a knack for coding or can collaborate with a developer, creating AI music tools, such as virtual instruments, melody generators, or rhythm creators, can be a lucrative venture. These tools can be marketed to amateur musicians, producers, and hobbyists seeking creative aids to enhance their compositions.

9.3.3. AI-Enhanced Music Production Services

Offering AI-powered services like mastering, mixing, or sound design can attract clients looking for high-quality production at competitive rates. Services like automated vocal tuning or AI-enhanced audio restoration can also be part of your offerings, allowing you to cater to a niche audience with specific needs.

9.3.4. Licensing AI-Composed Music

AI tools can rapidly produce music in various genres, making it easier for artists to create compositions that appeal to commercial clients. Licensing your AI-generated tracks for use in movies, TV shows, video games, and advertisements can become a steady source of income. Consider partnering with licensing platforms like AudioJungle or Epidemic Sound to reach a global audience.

9.3.5. Educational Resources and Consulting

Position yourself as a thought leader by sharing your expertise in AI music. Create and sell online courses, e-books, or webinars on how to use AI tools effectively in music production. Consulting services for studios, record labels, or individual artists interested in adopting AI in their workflow can also be a viable revenue stream.

9.3.6. NFTs and Digital Collectibles

Non-fungible tokens (NFTs) have revolutionized digital ownership. Selling AI-composed tracks, unique soundscapes, or personalized audio experiences as NFTs can tap into the growing market of digital art and collectibles. This approach allows fans to invest in your creativity while fostering a deeper connection with your audience.

9.3.7. Subscription Models for AI-Generated Content

A subscription-based service for access to exclusive AI-generated content, such as monthly packs of loops, stems, or customizable compositions, can build a consistent revenue stream. This model appeals to creators seeking fresh material for their projects on a regular basis.

By combining creativity with technology, AI offers a vast array of opportunities for monetizing your music career. As an AI musician, embracing these digital avenues can not only diversify your income but also establish your presence at the forefront of the industry's future.

Synthesized Sounds - A New Era

10- Networking in the Digital MusicEra

10.1 Importance of Building a Professional Network in the Industry

In the rapidly evolving landscape of the digital music era, establishing a robust professional network has become more critical than ever. As AI and technology reshape the music industry, the value of meaningful connections extends far beyond traditional roles. Networking offers unparalleled opportunities to collaborate, innovate, and stay ahead in an industry driven by creativity and technological breakthroughs.

A professional network acts as a gateway to resources, mentorship, and partnerships. By connecting with peers, producers, technologists, and industry leaders, individuals gain access to valuable insights, emerging trends, and potential collaborations that can significantly impact their career trajectory. For instance, an aspiring AI music composer might find collaborators to develop groundbreaking projects or mentors to refine their artistic and technical skills.

Moreover, in a competitive field like AI-driven music, where algorithms meet artistry, networking provides a platform to showcase talents and build credibility. Engaging in online communities, attending industry conferences, and participating in workshops allows professionals to build their personal brand and discover new opportunities. Platforms like LinkedIn, SoundCloud, and AI-focused forums have become modern arenas where music and tech enthusiasts converge, making it easier than ever to find like-minded individuals and industry experts.

Ultimately, building a professional network is about creating a support system that fosters growth and collaboration. In an era where music is synthesized with technology, the connections you cultivate today could be the stepping stones to tomorrow's innovations.

10.2 Utilizing Online Communities and Forums for Collaboration

In the rapidly evolving digital music landscape, online communities and forums have become invaluable resources for musicians, producers, and enthusiasts seeking collaboration. These platforms transcend geographical limitations, allowing artists from diverse backgrounds and expertise to connect, share ideas, and collaborate on projects in real-time.

10.2.1

The beauty of online communities lies in their ability to bring together like-minded individuals, regardless of location. Whether it's music production, sound design, or AI-driven composition, forums such as Reddit's music production subreddits, Gearslutz, or AI-specific forums like OpenAI's communities provide a fertile ground for exchange and collaboration. These platforms are often filled with professionals, hobbyists, and tech enthusiasts who actively contribute by offering tips, troubleshooting advice, and engaging in spirited discussions.

10.2.2

For AI music creators, communities centered around machine learning, algorithms, and data-driven composition can be particularly beneficial. Artists and developers often share code, patches, and tutorials that can be used to experiment and innovate, leading to breakthroughs that push the boundaries of creativity. These interactions not only foster individual growth but also open doors for joint ventures, where artists collaborate on developing new sounds or AI-based music projects.

10.2.3

Collaborating online through these forums can take many forms, from simple feedback exchanges to full-scale joint projects. Many platforms offer project collaboration tools, file sharing capabilities, and access to a vast pool of resources, enabling seamless teamwork. For example, platforms like Splice or Kompoz allow users to upload and work on tracks collaboratively, while also offering access to a library of sounds and loops created by other community members. These interactions often evolve into long-term partnerships that can help elevate an artist's career.

10.2.4

Importantly, online communities serve as platforms for networking, allowing musicians to build meaningful relationships with industry experts, peers, and even potential clients. By participating in discussions, offering helpful feedback, and showcasing one's work, individuals can enhance their visibility, gain recognition, and potentially secure collaborations with other professionals in the field.

Online communities and forums are not only powerful tools for learning and growing as a musician in the digital age, but they also serve as key avenues for networking and collaboration. As AI music continues to evolve, being an active participant in these spaces will provide artists with the opportunity to stay at the forefront of innovation while building relationships that can help accelerate their careers.

10.3 Attending Virtual and Live Music Industry Events for Connections

In the age of digital transformation, attending both virtual and live music industry events has become a crucial element for building lasting connections and advancing your career in AI-driven music. Whether it's an online webinar, a virtual conference, or an in-person music festival, these events provide unique opportunities to engage with key players in the industry, from record label executives and A&R professionals to fellow musicians and tech innovators.

Virtual events, in particular, have made networking more accessible than ever before. With the world becoming increasingly interconnected, you no longer have to travel long distances or incur high costs to meet industry experts and collaborators. Through virtual platforms, you can attend panel discussions, live Q&A sessions, and music industry webinars, all while sitting in the comfort of your home. These events often feature breakout rooms, chat features, and networking sessions that facilitate meaningful connections with like-minded professionals. Whether you are looking to collaborate on a project, seeking mentorship, or hoping to gain insights into the future of AI in music, these virtual touchpoints are invaluable for fostering relationships.

On the other hand, live music events, such as conferences, festivals, and expos, still hold significant power when it comes to face-to-face networking. There's an undeniable energy and personal touch that comes with in-person interactions, where the spontaneous nature of these gatherings can lead to more organic connections. Whether it's exchanging business cards, engaging in casual conversations with influential figures, or participating in industry-specific workshops, the chances of meeting collaborators, investors, or potential clients are far greater in these environments. Additionally, live events provide an immersive experience that combines music and technology, offering first and exposure to new AI-driven tools, platforms, and innovations that may be shaping the future of the industry.

To make the most out of both virtual and live events, it's essential to approach networking strategically. Prioritize events aligned with your career goals, research speakers and attendees beforehand, and take the time to introduce yourself and engage in meaningful conversations. Building your reputation through consistent and genuine networking will set the stage for collaboration, career growth, and greater visibility in the ever-evolving world of AI music.

"Networking is not just about collecting contacts; it's about building relationships that are mutually beneficial and long-lasting."

Synthesized Sounds - A New Era

11- Understanding Music Rights and Royalties

11.1 Breakdown of Music Rights: Authorship, Performance, and Distribution

In the evolving landscape of music, especially within the realm of AI-generated compositions, understanding the various rights associated with a piece of music is critical for both creators and business professionals in the industry. Music rights can be categorized into three primary areas: authorship, performance, and distribution. Each of these rights plays a pivotal role in how music is created, shared, and monetized.

11.1.1 Authorship Rights (Copyright)

➤ Authorship rights, also known as copyright, are granted to the creator of a musical work. This includes the lyrics, melody, composition, and arrangement. The person or entity who creates the original work automatically holds the copyright, which allows them to control how their music is used and the royalties generated from it. Copyright owners have the exclusive right to reproduce, distribute, perform, and create derivative works based on their creation.

➤ With AI music, the question of authorship becomes more complex. If an AI system generates a song, who owns the copyright: the creator of the AI, the developer of the algorithm, or the AI itself? Legal frameworks are still catching up with technological advances in AI music, making this an area that requires careful consideration.

11.1.2 Performance Rights (Public Performance)

➢ Performance rights are related to the live or public performance of a musical work. This includes concerts, radio broadcasts, television performances, and streaming platforms. Performance rights ensure that musicians, composers, and songwriters are compensated when their works are publicly performed or transmitted.

➢ In the case of AI-generated music, performance rights are typically held by the creator of the AI or the rights holder if the AI is used to reproduce or perform a piece of music in public settings. Performance Rights Organizations (PROs) such as ASCAP, BMI, and SESAC are responsible for managing these rights and distributing the royalties to the creators.

11.1.3 Distribution Rights

➢ Distribution rights concern the sale, licensing, and digital distribution of music. These rights determine how a piece of music is made available to the public, whether through physical formats (CDs, vinyl) or digital platforms (streaming services like Spotify, Apple Music, or downloads via iTunes). Distribution rights ensure that creators receive a fair share of royalties whenever their music is sold or streamed.

➢ As AI-generated music finds its way onto platforms, understanding the distribution rights becomes even more essential. If AI music is being distributed on streaming services, determining who gets compensated (and how) is crucial to the success and sustainability of the music business.

Synthesized Sounds - A New Era

Music distributors, record labels, and digital platforms typically handle these processes, but AI creators need to be mindful of the licensing agreements and the terms associated with distributing their work.

The breakdown of music rights into authorship, performance, and distribution forms the foundation of how royalties are generated and distributed. As AI-generated music becomes more prevalent, understanding these rights—and the complexities involved in their application—is essential for anyone looking to build a career in the new era of digital and synthesized sounds.

11.2 Navigating the Complexities of Music Royalties and Licensing

In the rapidly evolving landscape of AI-generated music, understanding the intricacies of music royalties and licensing is crucial for any artist or producer aiming to build a sustainable career. As the lines between traditional music creation and artificial intelligence blur, navigating this complex terrain requires a keen awareness of both legal frameworks and emerging industry practices.

Music royalties are financial compensations paid to creators, performers, and rights holders whenever their work is used commercially. These royalties typically fall into various categories, including performance royalties, mechanical royalties, synchronization royalties, and digital royalties.

However, with the rise of AI music production tools, these royalties often present unique challenges.

One key area of complexity is determining ownership. Who owns the rights to an AI-generated composition—the programmer of the AI, the user who creates the piece, or both? This is an open question that the music industry and legal systems are still grappling with. As AI continues to take a more active role in the creation process, understanding how ownership and credit are distributed will be crucial.

Furthermore, licensing is another critical aspect. Music licensing refers to the permissions granted for the use of copyrighted music in various formats, such as films, advertisements, or streaming services. AI-generated music adds another layer of

complexity to licensing agreements, as the traditional structures may need to be redefined to account for the involvement of machines in the creative process. It's essential for artists working with AI to explore how their works can be licensed across multiple platforms, ensuring they're properly compensated when their music is used commercially.

A solid understanding of these elements is not only vital for protecting your work but also for maximizing your earning potential. Whether you're a musician, a producer, or an entrepreneur venturing into AI music, learning how to navigate the complexities of music royalties and licensing will be an invaluable skill in today's digital-first music industry. Building a career in AI-generated music is not only about creativity—it's also about mastering the legal and financial tools that will help your career thrive.

11.3 Resources for Artists to Track and Claim Their Earnings

In the evolving landscape of AI-driven music production, artists need to be proactive in managing their rights and royalties. Fortunately, a range of digital tools and platforms have emerged, helping creators track and claim earnings efficiently. These resources offer transparency, ensuring that every stream, sale, or usage of their music is accounted for.

11.3.1- Performance Rights Organizations (PROs) PROs, such as ASCAP, BMI, and SESAC, play a crucial role in helping artists collect performance royalties. They track airplay, live performances, and digital streaming, ensuring that artists receive compensation for public usage of their music. By registering with these organizations, musicians can access regular updates about their earnings and royalties.

11.3.2- Digital Distribution Platforms Platforms like TuneCore, DistroKid, and CD Baby are vital for distributing music to streaming services like Spotify, Apple Music, and YouTube. These services often include dashboards where artists can monitor earnings in real-time, providing a transparent overview of revenue from streams, downloads, and sync licensing.

11.3.3- Music Royalty Tracking Software Software tools like Royalty Exchange and Songtrust help artists manage and track their music royalties across different revenue streams. Songtrust, for example, helps artists register their music with a variety of PROs and digital platforms, centralizing royalty payments and ensuring that every penny earned is tracked.

Synthesized Sounds - A New Era

11.3.4- Blockchain and Smart Contracts The emergence of blockchain technology has introduced a more direct, transparent way for artists to track their earnings. Platforms like Ujo Music and Audius utilize blockchain to manage and distribute royalties, ensuring that payments are made quickly and without the need for intermediaries. Smart contracts, integrated into blockchain platforms, can automate royalty payments based on predefined conditions, enhancing transparency.

11.3.5- Sync Licensing Platforms Platforms like Musicbed, Songtradr, and Artlist offer artists the opportunity to license their music for use in films, commercials, and TV shows. These platforms help track sync licensing deals and ensure that artists are compensated for their work in media production.

11.3.6- AI-powered Analytics Tools With the rise of AI, several analytics tools are now available that use machine learning to track an artist's music usage across digital platforms. Services like Audiam and MojiTrack provide automated, AI-driven insights into where and how music is being used across platforms, helping artists identify potential revenue streams that might have otherwise been overlooked.

By utilizing these resources, artists can better manage their careers in the age of AI music production, ensuring they are paid fairly and regularly for the creative work they produce.

12- The Role of AI in Music Education

12.1 Innovations in music learning through AI tools

The integration of Artificial Intelligence (AI) into music education is redefining the way students approach learning and mastering the art of music. AI tools are bringing significant innovations, offering personalized learning experiences that were once unimaginable. From beginner musicians to seasoned professionals, AI is providing transformative opportunities to enhance musical skills, creativity, and understanding.

One of the most notable innovations in music learning through AI is the development of intelligent tutoring systems. These systems are capable of providing real-time feedback, adjusting lesson plans based on the student's progress, and offering targeted exercises that address specific areas of difficulty. Whether learning an instrument or voice training, AI-powered platforms such as Yousician and Flowkey use machine learning algorithms to evaluate a student's performance, detect errors, and offer suggestions for improvement. This personalized approach accelerates learning and fosters self-paced growth.

Furthermore, AI is enhancing the ability to learn complex music theory concepts in an engaging and intuitive manner. Programs like SmartMusic and Musicoach allow students to practice sight-reading, rhythm exercises, and even music composition with an AI companion that adapts to their skill level. These tools are instrumental in bridging the gap between theory and practice, enabling learners to not only understand but also apply complex music concepts.

Synthesized Sounds - A New Era

Another major breakthrough is the use of AI for composition and songwriting. AI-powered software such as Aiva and Amper Music allows budding composers to generate musical ideas, experiment with different styles, and compose pieces that reflect a variety of genres. For students aspiring to build a career in music, these tools offer a safe space to explore their creativity and produce original works without the constraints of traditional methods.

With AI as a co-creator, musicians can focus more on their artistic expression while letting the AI handle repetitive tasks, such as generating harmonies or creating chord progressions. The collaboration between human musicians and AI is also pushing the boundaries of performance. AI can assist in orchestrating and arranging music, as well as enhance live performances by synchronizing with musicians, creating dynamic backing tracks, or even adjusting real-time sound design based on audience interaction. These innovations are reshaping the performance aspect of music education by merging the technical with the artistic.

Moreover, AI-powered music recognition tools are revolutionizing music appreciation and education. Through platforms like Musixmatch and Shazam, students and educators can instantly identify songs, study their structure, and even learn how specific techniques are applied. This technology enriches the learning experience by providing students with a deeper understanding of the songs they study, offering a more interactive and analytical approach to music appreciation.

In the context of AI's evolving role in music education, students can also benefit from AI-driven assessment tools that evaluate not just the technical accuracy of a piece, but also the expressiveness and emotional depth of the performance. These tools help students develop a more holistic understanding of their musicality, which is crucial in the development of their artistry.

AI tools are revolutionizing music education, offering innovative ways for students to learn, practice, compose, and perform music. As we move further into the AI era, these tools will continue to evolve, paving the way for future musicians to develop their craft in ways that merge tradition with cutting-edge technology. For those looking to build a career in AI music, these innovations present exciting opportunities to explore new frontiers in both the creation and appreciation of music.

12.2 Online Courses and Platforms for Aspiring Musicians

In the age of AI-driven innovation, aspiring musicians have access to a wealth of resources that were once unavailable. Online courses and platforms have become indispensable tools for musicians looking to build their careers in the evolving music industry. These platforms offer a blend of traditional learning with the flexibility of modern technology, enabling students to learn at their own pace while integrating the latest in music production tools, including AI.

12.2.1 Music Production and Theory Courses
  ➤ Platforms like Coursera, Udemy, and Skillshare host a variety of music courses, ranging from basic music theory to advanced production techniques. These courses are often taught by industry professionals,

providing a practical and theoretical foundation for musicians. Many platforms now incorporate AI-driven learning systems, which adapt the curriculum to the student's progress and offer personalized learning paths.

12.2.2. AI-Powered Music Software Tutorials

➢ Music production software such as Ableton Live, Logic Pro, and FL Studio, now often integrates AI features that help with mixing, mastering, and sound generation. Many online platforms offer in-depth tutorials on how to use these tools effectively, allowing musicians to stay at the forefront of new technological developments in music creation. These tutorials cover everything from the basic layout of the software to more advanced techniques like AI-assisted composition.

12.2.3. Interactive Platforms for Collaboration

➢ AI is also transforming how musicians collaborate. Platforms like Splice, BandLab, and Kompoz have embraced AI technology to assist with music production and provide virtual spaces where musicians can work together regardless of geographical location. These platforms facilitate collaboration through cloud-based music production tools that use AI algorithms to help with the synchronization of different musical elements, harmonization, and arrangement.

12.2.4. AI Music Analysis and Feedback

➢ AI platforms such as Amper Music, AIVA, and Jukedeck are empowering musicians with AI-driven composition tools. These platforms allow creators to

Synthesized Sounds - A New Era

input ideas and get instant feedback on melody, harmony, and rhythm, helping them refine their compositions. By leveraging AI to analyze music trends and provide data-driven suggestions, these platforms enable musicians to create pieces that resonate with their target audiences.

12.2.5. Music Education Communities and Networking

➢ Communities such as MasterClass, YouTube, and Discord allow aspiring musicians to interact with other creators and professionals, exchanging knowledge and experiences. With AI algorithms now capable of recommending music tutorials, networking opportunities, and collaboration possibilities, aspiring musicians can expand their horizons and forge meaningful connections.

Online platforms for aspiring musicians are rapidly evolving, with AI playing a crucial role in enhancing learning experiences, enabling real-time feedback, and fostering collaboration. These resources not only make music education more accessible but also equip musicians with the technical skills and creative freedom to thrive in an AI-powered musical landscape.

12.3 Community and Mentorship Opportunities in AI-Facilitated Education

In the rapidly evolving world of AI in music education, the role of community and mentorship becomes indispensable. As technology progresses, music educators and students need not only access to innovative tools but also the guidance and support of experienced professionals to navigate this dynamic field. AI-facilitated education opens up unique opportunities for both community collaboration and mentorship, creating an ecosystem of shared learning and innovation.

12.3.1 AI-Powered Communities for Collaborative Learning

➢ AI has revolutionized how we connect, learn, and share in the world of music. Online platforms utilizing AI can bring together aspiring musicians, educators, and technologists to form communities that engage in collaborative learning. For instance, AI-driven tools like virtual collaboration spaces or music composition software enable individuals across the globe to work together in real time, regardless of geographical constraints. Communities formed in these spaces allow students to collaborate on projects, exchange ideas, and create original music in a way that fosters creativity and inclusivity. These communities, empowered by AI, ensure that even those with limited access to traditional institutions can participate and learn at their own pace.

12.3.2. Mentorship in the Age of Artificial Intelligence

➢ Mentorship remains a cornerstone of career development, and AI-facilitated education is amplifying this. AI algorithms can analyze students' progress, identifying strengths and areas for improvement. This data can then be used by mentors to offer personalized guidance tailored to each student's unique learning style. Moreover, AI can assist mentors by providing insights and feedback on the student's music compositions, performance skills, and technical knowledge. Mentorship in AI-powered environments can extend beyond one-on-one sessions; virtual mentorship programs can reach a broader audience, creating a scalable model where students can receive expert advice from professionals worldwide.

12.3.3. Building a Network Through AI-Inclusive Platforms

➢ AI-facilitated platforms not only allow students to learn but also to build their professional networks. Through these platforms, aspiring music professionals can connect with industry experts, seasoned educators, and fellow musicians. Networks built within AI-driven environments offer avenues for career development and real-time feedback, helping students secure internships, collaborations, and other career-enhancing opportunities. These platforms act as gateways to the music industry, providing a space for the next generation of musicians and technologists to grow, find support, and share their work with a global audience.

12.3.4. Personalized Growth Through AI-Tailored Mentorship

➢ AI has the potential to deliver highly personalized mentorship experiences. Machine learning algorithms can track a student's progress over time and suggest specific resources, lessons, or practices that align with their goals and current level of expertise. This dynamic approach ensures that each student's path is uniquely tailored to their needs. With AI, mentorship is no longer a one-size-fits-all experience; it adapts as the student evolves, providing them with real-time, actionable feedback that accelerates their learning and skill development.

Synthesized Sounds - A New Era

12.3.5. Bridging Gaps in Music Education with AI

➢ AI-driven communities and mentorship programs also play a critical role in democratizing access to music education. These technologies break down traditional barriers, making quality education more accessible to students in underserved regions or those without access to expensive, conventional music schools. Through AI, educational content can be distributed freely and efficiently, empowering a diverse range of students to pursue careers in music and technology.

The integration of community and mentorship opportunities in AI-facilitated music education is paving the way for a new generation of musicians and professionals. These networks of collaboration, feedback, and personalized guidance are crucial for building a sustainable career in the ever-evolving intersection of tunes and tech. By harnessing the power of AI, we create a future where music education is not only innovative but inclusive and supportive, ultimately enriching the field of music and technology alike.

Synthesized Sounds - A New Era

13- Trends Shaping The Future of AI Music

13.1 Identification of Emerging Trends in AI Music Technology

As artificial intelligence continues to evolve, its intersection with music technology has opened up new possibilities, reshaping the landscape of music creation, production, and consumption. One of the most exciting developments in this domain is the rapid emergence of AI-driven tools and platforms that enable artists, composers, and producers to create music in entirely novel ways.

13.1.1. AI as a Collaborative Tool

➢ Rather than replacing musicians, AI is becoming an invaluable collaborator in the creative process. Platforms like OpenAI's MuseNet and Jukedeck leverage deep learning algorithms to compose music in various genres, providing users with a musical foundation to build upon. Emerging trends in AI music technology suggest that this collaborative aspect will continue to grow, allowing for more dynamic and intuitive human-AI partnerships in music creation.

13.1.2. Real-Time Music Composition and Performance

➢ Another exciting trend is the development of AI systems capable of composing and performing music in real time. These AI tools adapt to human inputs and create compositions on the fly, blending improvisation with algorithmic precision. As AI technology matures, we can expect live performances by AI-driven music ensembles that respond to the nuances of audience interaction, creating a highly immersive and dynamic musical experience.

13.1.3. Personalized Music Experiences

➤ AI's ability to analyze user preferences and listening habits is paving the way for hyper-personalized music experiences. AI algorithms can curate playlists and recommend music tailored to individual tastes, moods, and even physiological states. In addition, AI tools are beginning to allow users to personalize compositions in real-time by adjusting elements such as tempo, instrumentation, and structure to suit their emotional or artistic needs.

13.1.4. Music Production and Mastering Automation

➤ The AI-driven automation of music production processes, such as mixing, mastering, and sound design, is another trend gaining traction. AI-powered tools can analyze the raw tracks and apply professional-grade sound engineering techniques, enhancing the overall quality of the music with minimal human intervention. This automation lowers the barriers to entry for aspiring music producers and enables established artists to focus more on the creative aspects of music making.

13.1.5. AI-Generated Music for Film, TV, and Advertising

➤ In addition to personal music creation, AI is making significant inroads into commercial and media music production. AI-driven music systems are being employed to generate custom soundtracks for films, TV shows, and advertisements, with the ability to craft scores that match specific emotions, themes, and pacing. The scalability and efficiency of AI in producing high-quality music for media is revolutionizing industries that rely on audio-visual content.

13.1.6. Ethical and Legal Implications

➢ As AI-generated music continues to gain prominence, questions surrounding intellectual property, ownership, and authorship will become increasingly important. Determining who owns the rights to music created by AI, as well as the ethical implications of using AI to replicate human creativity, is an ongoing challenge. The music industry will likely need to adapt to new legal frameworks and ethical standards as these AI technologies become more integrated into the creative process.

The identification of emerging trends in AI music technology points to an exciting future where creativity, technology, and collaboration converge in new and unexpected ways. As AI tools become more sophisticated, the boundaries of what is possible in music creation, production, and consumption will expand, offering new opportunities for musicians, composers, producers, and even audiences to experience music in innovative ways.

13.2 Predictions for Future Developments and Opportunities

The future of AI in music is poised to be transformative, unlocking countless opportunities for both creators and the industry at large. As artificial intelligence continues to evolve, the synergy between human creativity and

machine learning will likely lead to new genres, innovative production techniques, and unprecedented levels of personalization in music.

13.2.1

One of the key predictions for the future of AI music is the further democratization of music creation. With advancements in AI algorithms, even individuals with limited technical knowledge will be able to compose, produce, and perform music. We are already witnessing the rise of AI-driven tools that assist in the composition process, from melody generation to full arrangements. These tools will likely become more intuitive, accessible, and cost-effective, allowing musicians to bring their ideas to life faster and more efficiently.

13.2.2

Another area of potential growth lies in AI's ability to enhance personalization. The integration of AI-driven recommendation systems with music streaming platforms will allow for hyper-tailored listening experiences. By analyzing not only listening habits but also emotional responses and personal preferences, AI will curate playlists and suggest new artists that feel more relevant to each listener. This could lead to a deeper emotional connection with music and spur the discovery of niche genres and independent artists.

13.2.3

In addition to personalization, AI is likely to revolutionize the live performance space. The future may see AI-generated music accompanying live performers, creating a more immersive experience for audiences. Real-time music generation during concerts or festivals could lead to performances that are unique to each event, making every show a one-of-a-kind experience.

Synthesized Sounds - A New Era

13.2.4

As AI music tools become more sophisticated, we can also expect an increasing number of collaborations between AI systems and human artists. These collaborations will push the boundaries of creativity, offering opportunities for musicians to explore unfamiliar territory and experiment with novel sounds.

13.2.5

Furthermore, AI's ability to analyze vast amounts of music data could inspire new compositions by identifying trends and patterns that human artists might otherwise overlook.

In terms of career opportunities, the growth of AI music will provide new avenues for professionals to engage with the industry. Musicians can explore careers as AI composers, sound designers, and developers of AI music software. Additionally, music producers, sound engineers, and even marketers will find new opportunities as the tools and platforms powered by AI expand. There will also be a surge in demand for AI music curators and consultants who can help businesses and artists navigate the evolving landscape.

13.2.6

While challenges remain, such as the ethical considerations surrounding AI-generated music and intellectual property, the future looks promising for AI in music. Those willing to embrace this technological evolution will find that the possibilities are not only limitless but also a fertile ground for innovation, artistic expression, and entrepreneurial endeavors. As we move forward into the next era of music creation, the fusion of technology and art will continue to shape the way we experience music, offering infinite possibilities for both the creators and consumers of this ever-evolving art form.

13.3 How These Trends Will Impact Musicians and the Industry?

The rise of AI in music creation has sparked a revolution in how music is composed, produced, and consumed. These advancements bring with them significant implications for musicians and the industry as a whole, reshaping the roles of artists, producers, and even listeners.

13.3.1

For musicians, AI will serve as both a tool and a collaborator. AI-driven music software can assist artists in composing, arranging, and mixing, allowing them to focus more on their creative vision. These tools will democratize music production, enabling independent artists to create high-quality tracks without the need for expensive equipment or studio time. For emerging artists, AI will provide access to a level of musical expertise and production quality that was once reserved for top-tier professionals. AI can generate musical ideas, suggest chord progressions, or even automate repetitive tasks like mastering, allowing musicians to streamline their workflows and expand their creative possibilities.

13.3.2

However, as AI becomes a more integral part of the production process, the traditional roles within the industry may evolve. Producers, sound engineers, and even session musicians might see a shift in demand as AI tools become more capable of automating many aspects of music production. This will lead to a more efficient industry, but could also result in job displacement, especially for roles that rely on routine tasks.

13.3.3

For the broader music industry, these changes will likely have profound effects on how music is marketed and distributed. AI can analyze listener preferences and trends, offering more personalized recommendations and insights into consumer behavior. This can help record labels, streaming platforms, and independent artists make more informed decisions about which tracks to release and how to target specific audiences. Additionally, AI's ability to generate music on demand could lead to the rise of adaptive soundtracks, where music is tailored to the listener's mood or environment in real-time.

13.3.4

While AI presents exciting opportunities for innovation, it also raises questions around creativity, ownership, and ethics. As AI systems become more adept at mimicking human creativity, there will be growing concerns about authorship: who owns the music generated by an AI? How should royalties be distributed when an AI contributes to the composition process? These questions will challenge the legal and ethical frameworks of the music industry, requiring new policies and agreements to address the complexities of AI-generated works.

AI's influence on the music industry will be transformative, providing musicians with new opportunities to create and innovate. However, it will also necessitate a shift in how music is produced, consumed, and valued. Musicians who embrace these trends and adapt to the evolving landscape will be well-positioned to thrive in this new era of music.

Synthesized Sounds - A New Era

14- *Preparing for the AI Future of Music*

14.1 Skills that will be essential for future musicians

➢ In the ever-evolving landscape of music, fueled by rapid advancements in artificial intelligence (AI) and technology, the future musician must develop a hybrid skill set that blends artistry with technical acumen. As we transition into a new era of sound creation, where AI plays a pivotal role in music production, musicians must equip themselves with both traditional musical skills and a deep understanding of technological tools. The following skills will be critical for musicians navigating this AI-powered future:

14.1.1 Proficiency in Music Production Software and AI Tools

➢ Musicians of the future will need to master a variety of music production platforms, ranging from industry-standard Digital Audio Workstations (DAWs) to specialized AI-driven tools. Knowledge of AI-powered software for music composition, mastering, and sound design will allow musicians to expand their creative boundaries while optimizing production efficiency.

14.1.2 Data Literacy and Algorithmic Understanding

➢ AI systems often require musicians to work with algorithms, data analysis, and machine learning models that can predict, enhance, and even compose music. Future musicians should understand how these algorithms work, from neural networks to generative adversarial networks (GANs), and how they can leverage these tools to co-create music alongside AI.

Synthesized Sounds - A New Era

14.1.3 Adaptability to New Technologies

➢ The pace at which new technologies are shaping the music industry means that musicians must embrace a mindset of continual learning. Emerging technologies, such as virtual reality (VR) for live performances, augmented reality (AR) for immersive sound experiences, and blockchain for music rights management, will all require musicians to stay adaptable and open to innovation.

14.1.4 Collaboration with AI and Cross-Disciplinary Partnerships

➢ The future of music lies not only in the hands of human musicians but also in collaboration with AI. Musicians will need to learn how to work seamlessly with AI systems, using them as creative partners rather than competitors. Additionally, there will be increased opportunities for collaboration across disciplines, such as combining music with gaming, film, or interactive media, creating new forms of artistic expression.

14.1.5 Critical Thinking and Curation

➢ With AI capable of generating an endless array of musical content, the human touch will be required for the curation and refinement of sound. Musicians will need to apply critical thinking to select, interpret, and personalize AI-generated music to create unique compositions that resonate with audiences on a deeper level.

Synthesized Sounds - A New Era

14.1.6 Business Acumen and Digital Marketing Skills

➢ The rise of digital platforms and social media, combined with AI's role in shaping music distribution, calls for musicians to become proficient in marketing and branding themselves. Understanding digital rights management (DRM), monetization strategies, and how to leverage AI tools for social media engagement will be pivotal for building a sustainable career in the new music economy.

14.1.7 Understanding of Ethics and Intellectual Property

➢ As AI begins to generate music autonomously, questions of authorship, copyright, and intellectual property will become increasingly important. Musicians will need a solid understanding of intellectual property laws and ethical issues surrounding AI-created music to ensure fair use and protect their creative work.

14.1.8 Emotional Intelligence and Storytelling

➢ While AI can mimic and generate melodies, harmonies, and rhythms, it is the human element that will continue to bring meaning, emotion, and context to music. Musicians will need to develop emotional intelligence to connect with audiences on a deeper, more personal level through storytelling, both in their music and through the content they create around it.

As we look toward the future of music, it is clear that AI will play a transformative role in shaping the industry. However, the unique creative potential of human musicians will remain indispensable. By embracing these skills, musicians can ensure their relevance in this exciting new chapter of music history, blending art and technology in ways that were once unimaginable.

Synthesized Sounds - A New Era

14.2 The Importance of Adaptability in a Changing Industry

The music industry is undergoing a transformation unlike any seen before. With the rise of artificial intelligence (AI), we are witnessing new technological advancements that have the potential to reshape how music is created, produced, and experienced. For musicians, producers, and industry professionals, this means that adaptability is no longer a luxury-it's a necessity.

14.2.1

As AI tools continue to evolve, they are rapidly altering the landscape of music production. From generative music algorithms to AI-driven mastering tools, professionals are presented with unprecedented opportunities to innovate and enhance their craft. However, this also means the traditional ways of working are being challenged. For individuals and companies to thrive in this new environment, they must be agile and open to learning new skills, embracing new technologies, and exploring unfamiliar creative avenues.

14.2.2

Adaptability in the face of this change involves more than just technological competence. It requires a shift in mindset. Those who are successful in AI-driven music careers will be the ones who view AI not as a threat but as an ally an instrument to push the boundaries of their creativity. Whether it's experimenting with AI to generate novel compositions or leveraging machine learning to optimize the listening experience, the future belongs to those who remain flexible and eager to adapt.

14.2.3

Moreover, adaptability in this context means understanding the changing business models, audience expectations, and distribution platforms that AI is influencing. As AI tools democratize music creation, aspiring professionals must learn to navigate new ecosystems that blur the lines between artist and technologist. The music industry is now more accessible to those who can blend the art of music with the science of technology.

14.2.4

This era will favor the multi-disciplinary professional—one who understands the potential of both creativity and computation.

In the chapters ahead, we will explore how to build a career in this rapidly evolving space, with a focus on staying relevant, adaptable, and ahead of the curve. The AI future of music may be unknown, but with the right mindset, the possibilities are endless.

14.3 Continuous Learning and Staying Ahead in Technology

As we stand on the cusp of a new era in music creation, driven by AI, it is essential to recognize the importance of continuous learning. The AI landscape in the music industry is constantly evolving, and staying ahead requires a commitment to staying informed and adaptable. This is especially true for those seeking to build careers in AI music, where the tools, techniques, and applications are changing rapidly.

14.3.1

Technological advancements are redefining how music is composed, produced, and even consumed. From machine learning algorithms that can generate complex melodies to AI systems capable of mastering tracks in seconds, the possibilities are endless. However, this also means that today's cutting-edge technology will soon become outdated, and tomorrow's innovations will require new knowledge and skills.

14.3.2

For those looking to thrive in this space, a mindset of lifelong learning is crucial. Staying updated with the latest AI research papers, attending conferences, joining online communities, and taking courses will be key to mastering the tools that will shape the future of music. Engaging with industry leaders and collaborating with fellow professionals can also provide invaluable insights into the direction AI is heading and how to leverage it to create new musical experiences.

14.3.3

Moreover, practical experience is just as vital. Experimenting with AI-powered music tools, participating in hackathons, and even collaborating with tech developers can provide hands-on knowledge that theoretical learning cannot match. By actively engaging in the technological advancements around AI music, you can develop the necessary skills to stay relevant and innovative in this rapidly transforming field.

In the AI-driven future of music, those who continuously adapt and evolve will be the ones who shape the soundscape of tomorrow. So, embrace learning, stay curious, and prepare to lead the charge in creating the next generation of music.

Synthesized Sounds - A New Era

15- Overcoming Creative Blocks with AI

15.1 Techniques for Using AI to Inspire and Break Through Writer's Block

Writer's block is a frustrating and often paralyzing experience for any musician or creator. In the realm of AI music, it can feel like the well of creativity has run dry, leaving the artist stuck in a loop of indecision and stalled progress. Fortunately, AI can act as a powerful tool to help break free from these creative barriers and reignite the flow of ideas. By leveraging AI in various forms, musicians can find inspiration, explore new musical territories, and overcome the limitations that writer's block can impose.

15.1.1. AI-Powered Generators for New Ideas
➢ AI-driven platforms can offer fresh melodies, chord progressions, and rhythm patterns that can spark new directions in composition. These tools analyze vast libraries of existing music to suggest novel combinations, helping to push boundaries that might feel unreachable. For example, an AI music generator can provide a set of motifs based on a genre or mood you're aiming for, giving you a foundation on which to build.

15.1.2. AI as a Co-Creator: Collaborative Composition
➢ Sometimes, collaboration with AI can provide the external perspective needed to overcome creative block. Many AI systems allow musicians to start a composition and then invite the AI to finish it or offer variations. This collaboration can feel like working

with a bandmate who challenges your ideas and brings out the best in your creativity, especially when you feel stuck.

15.1.3. Mood-Based AI Composition Tools

➤ AI tools that respond to mood and emotion can help you navigate through moments of creative frustration. These tools analyze emotional cues in your input and use algorithms to craft compositions that match or challenge your emotional state. This approach encourages experimentation and can lead to breakthroughs when your creative energy feels blocked.

15.1.4. Randomization and Parameter Tweaking

➤ AI can help introduce elements of randomness into your music-making process. By tweaking certain parameters like tempo, key, or instrumentation, AI can help you explore music in unexpected ways. It's a useful technique for shaking off the rigidity of perfectionism and opening up to more playful, spontaneous creativity.

15.1.5. AI-Assisted Lyrics Generation

➤ For composers who focus on songwriting, AI lyric generators can be invaluable. By inputting a theme, mood, or even a few lines, you can prompt an AI to generate lyrics that align with your vision, which might inspire your next verse or chorus. By offering unexpected lyrical directions, AI can break through the stagnation that often accompanies the blank page.

15.1.6. AI for Sound Exploration and Design

> ➤ Sound design can also be a source of writer's block. AI-based sound exploration tools can generate unique soundscapes that trigger new ideas for compositions.

By using AI to manipulate samples, layers, and effects, musicians can access complex textures and new sonic possibilities that inspire fresh creative visions.

15.1.7. Music Analysis for Growth

> ➤ AI can analyze your previous works and suggest patterns, structures, or techniques that you might not have considered before. By drawing attention to recurring elements or underused musical devices, AI can push you to explore new directions in your compositions. This analysis can be a helpful reminder that even in moments of doubt, your past work holds a wealth of ideas waiting to be rediscovered.

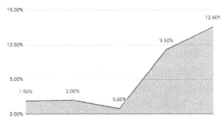

By integrating AI into the creative process, musicians can turn the challenge of writer's block into an opportunity for growth and innovation. AI offers not only practical tools but also a mindset shift: rather than seeing it as a crutch, musicians can use AI as a way to tap into deeper levels of creativity, breaking through barriers and achieving a new flow of inspiration.

15.2 Tools Available for Generating Ideas and Musical Motifs

When facing creative blocks, technology offers powerful tools to spark inspiration and craft musical ideas. AI-driven platforms have emerged as a vital resource for musicians and producers, allowing them to explore uncharted territories in sound design, composition, and arrangement. Here are some key tools available for generating ideas and musical motifs:

15.2.1. AI-Powered Composition Software
➢ Tools like OpenAI's MuseNet and AIVA (Artificial Intelligence Virtual Artist) use machine learning to generate melodies, chord progressions, and even entire compositions. These platforms analyze vast datasets of musical styles and genres, offering customized outputs based on user preferences.

15.2.2. Digital Audio Workstations (DAWs) with AI Integration
➢ DAWs like Ableton Live, FL Studio, and Logic Pro now integrate AI plugins that suggest chord progressions, rhythmic patterns, and instrument choices. Tools such as Captain Plugins and Scaler assist in creating harmonic frameworks tailored to your creative vision.

15.2.3. Generative Sequencers and Synthesizers
➢ Generative music tools, like Output's Arcade and Roli's Equator, allow artists to create evolving motifs by manipulating parameters. These tools are

Synthesized Sounds - A New Era

particularly useful for electronic music, enabling endless variations of loops and textures.

15.2.4. AI-Based Sample Libraries and Remix Tools
➢ Platforms like Splice and Loopcloud leverage AI to recommend samples and loops that complement your project. AI remix tools, such as Endlesss and Algonaut Atlas, help deconstruct tracks and remix them into entirely new ideas.

15.2.5. Lyric and Melody Generators
➢ AI-powered lyric generators like LyricStudio and tools like Humtap, which create melodies from your humming or singing, offer a quick way to jumpstart creative ideas when you're stuck.

15.2.6. Collaborative AI Platforms
➢ Services like Amper Music and Boomy facilitate co-creation with AI, enabling you to create royalty-free tracks by selecting mood, tempo, and genre. These platforms are excellent for producers looking to develop ideas rapidly.

Incorporating these tools into your workflow not only enhances creativity but also allows for experimentation with styles and techniques that may be outside your comfort zone. By embracing AI as a collaborator, musicians can overcome creative blocks and unlock a world of sonic possibilities.

Synthesized Sounds - A New Era

15.3 The Psychological Aspects of Creative Work and Technology

In the realm of creative work, particularly in music, the mind often becomes both a source of inspiration and a formidable barrier. The psychological aspects of creativity are a labyrinth of emotions, ideas, and self-reflections. While moments of brilliance can propel an artist forward, periods of self-doubt, anxiety, and creative stagnation commonly known as creative blocks can hinder progress and lead to frustration.

15.3.1
Technology, particularly artificial intelligence, has emerged as a transformative tool for overcoming these challenges. At its core, AI serves as both a collaborator and a muse, offering fresh perspectives and breaking patterns that may confine an artist's thought process. By analyzing vast datasets of music and generating novel combinations of sound, AI helps musicians explore uncharted creative territories. This collaboration reduces the psychological burden of starting from scratch or facing the "blank canvas" syndrome, which can often paralyze even the most seasoned creators.

15.3.2
Moreover, AI-driven tools can alleviate perfectionism, a common psychological barrier. These tools provide immediate feedback, offering iterative improvements and encouraging experimentation without fear of judgment. The ability to quickly prototype and refine ideas fosters a sense of progress, which is crucial in maintaining motivation and combating the self-doubt that frequently accompanies creative work.

Synthesized Sounds - A New Era

15.3.3

From a broader perspective, integrating AI into creative workflows addresses the psychological need for novelty and challenge. The unpredictability of AI-generated outputs can reawaken a sense of curiosity and playfulness, helping artists reconnect with the joy of creation. It shifts the focus from a fear of failure to a mindset of exploration and growth.

In Synthesized Sounds: A New Era, the interplay between human creativity and AI highlights not just a technological revolution but a psychological one. By leveraging AI to overcome mental blocks, artists are not only reclaiming their creative agency but also transforming the way music is conceptualized and produced. This marriage of tunes and tech signals a promising future for those willing to embrace this new frontier in AI music.

Synthesized Sounds - A New Era

16- Overcoming Creative Blocks with AI

16.1 Profile of the Self-Sufficient Artist in the Digital Age

The self-sufficient artist of the digital age is a fascinating blend of creativity, technical acumen, and entrepreneurial spirit. In an era defined by rapid technological advancements, the modern musician is no longer solely an artist but also a strategist, technologist, and marketer. This transformation is particularly pronounced in the world of AI-powered music creation, where tools and platforms empower individuals to compose, produce, and distribute music without the traditional infrastructure of recording studios, managers, or labels.

16.1.1 Characteristics of the Digital-Age Musician
16.1.1.1. Creative Technologists:
> ➤ These artists leverage AI-powered tools for composition, sound design, and mastering. Software like AI-driven DAWs (Digital Audio Workstations) and virtual assistants for music production allow them to experiment with genres and styles that were once constrained by human limitations.

16.1.1.2. Entrepreneurial Mindsets:
> ➤ The DIY musician thrives on self-management. They understand the importance of personal branding, monetization strategies, and community building. Platforms like Bandcamp, Patreon, and TikTok become their stages, enabling direct interaction with fans while earning revenue independently.

16.1.1.3. Agility and Adaptability:

➢ In a constantly evolving technological landscape, adaptability is key. These musicians remain students of innovation, regularly updating their skill sets to stay ahead of trends, whether by learning AI programming basics or exploring new distribution methods like NFTs and blockchain-backed royalties.

16.1.1.4. Collaborative Independence:

➢ While self-sufficient, they embrace collaboration through global networks. Online communities of producers, vocalists, and sound engineers allow these artists to co-create and thrive in virtual studios, breaking geographical and financial barriers.

16.1.2 The Role of AI in Enabling Independence

➢ AI tools democratize music production, making professional-grade tools accessible to all. From generating entire tracks based on mood inputs to customizing soundscapes with minimal technical expertise, AI reduces the reliance on traditional gatekeepers. Moreover, automated distribution platforms and analytics tools empower artists to make data-driven decisions, optimizing their reach and impact.

The self-sufficient artist of the digital age is more than a musician—they are a curator of experiences, a storyteller empowered by technology, and a pioneer in a new era where creativity and technology intersect seamlessly. For these artists, independence isn't just a choice; it's a movement reshaping the music industry's future.

16.2 Resources for Producing Music Independently Using AI Tools

In the ever-evolving landscape of music production, artificial intelligence (AI) has emerged as a transformative force, empowering DIY musicians to produce professional-quality music independently. AI tools simplify complex processes, democratize access to cutting-edge technology, and provide creative solutions for artists at any stage of their career. Here are some essential resources for leveraging AI in music production:

16.2.1. AI-Powered Composition Tools
 ➤ AI composition tools assist musicians in creating melodies, harmonies, and full tracks, serving as both inspiration and collaboration partners. Tools like **AIVA** (Artificial Intelligence Virtual Artist) and **Amper Music** enable artists to compose genre-specific tracks with minimal effort. By customizing tempo, mood, and instrumentation, musicians can experiment with unique sounds.

16.2.2. AI-Driven Sound Design
 ➤ Crafting unique soundscapes and effects has never been easier. AI platforms like **Endlesss** and **LANDR Samples** offer extensive libraries of AI-curated samples, loops, and effects, providing infinite possibilities for sound design. Tools such as **Google's NSynth** use machine learning to create entirely new instruments by blending audio characteristics of existing sounds.

Synthesized Sounds - A New Era

16.2.3. Automated Mixing and Mastering Services

➢ Mixing and mastering are critical steps in music production that traditionally require expertise and expensive studio equipment. AI-powered platforms like **LANDR, CloudBounce,** and **eMastered** automate these processes, offering high-quality results tailored to your track's specific needs. These tools save time and money while maintaining professional standards.

16.2.4. AI Vocal Assistance and Generation

➢ Vocal production is another area where AI excels. Tools such as **Vocaloid** and **Synthesizer V** allow musicians to generate realistic or stylized vocal tracks without hiring a vocalist. For enhancing recorded vocals, plugins like **iZotope Nectar** use AI to refine pitch, tone, and overall performance effortlessly.

16.2.5. AI for Lyric Writing and Ideation

➢ Struggling with writer's block? AI-powered lyric generation tools like **Jarvis** (now **Jasper AI**) and **LyricStudio** can help you brainstorm themes, verses, or entire songs. These platforms are ideal for sparking creativity and exploring new lyrical directions.

16.2.6. Collaboration Platforms and Virtual Bands

➢ Online platforms like **Endlesss** enable real-time, collaborative music creation with artists worldwide. AI facilitates seamless collaboration by suggesting complementary elements and improving workflow, making it easier to co-create regardless of physical distance.

Synthesized Sounds - A New Era

16.2.7. Education and Skill Development
➢ Many AI tools come with built-in tutorials and learning modules. Platforms like **BandLab** and **Soundtrap** are beginner-friendly and incorporate AI features for composing, editing, and mixing. Additionally, online learning platforms like **Coursera** and **Udemy** offer courses on AI-driven music production.

16.2.8. Community and Support
➢ AI-powered music communities provide opportunities to learn, share, and grow. Forums like **r/WeAreTheMusicMakers** on Reddit or dedicated groups for tools like AIVA and LANDR allow musicians to exchange ideas, troubleshoot, and showcase their creations.

Empowering the Independent Musician
AI tools are leveling the playing field for independent musicians, providing access to technology once reserved for major studios.

By integrating these tools into their workflow, DIY artists can achieve creative freedom, save resources, and produce music that resonates with global audiences.

As the world of AI-driven music continues to expand, the DIY musician stands at the forefront of this new era, where tunes meet technology to redefine the music industry.

16.3 Strategies for Self-Promotion and Audience Engagement

In the ever-evolving landscape of the music industry, AI tools have revolutionized how independent musicians can promote themselves and engage with their audience. For DIY musicians, mastering these strategies is essential for standing out in a competitive market. Below are some key approaches tailored for the AI-driven era:

16.3.1. Leverage AI-Powered Marketing Tools
> ➢ AI tools like personalized email marketing platforms and AI-driven content schedulers can optimize when and where your content is shared. These platforms analyze audience behavior, enabling you to create customized marketing campaigns that resonate with your listeners.

Example: Use AI-powered platforms like Mailchimp to send newsletters tailored to individual fan preferences or automate social media posts for maximum reach using tools like Buffer or Hootsuite.

16.3.2. Create Immersive Experiences with AI
> ➢ AI tools can help you create interactive and engaging experiences. Virtual reality (VR) concerts, AI-generated album art, or interactive AI-powered music experiences can captivate your audience and differentiate your brand.

Example: Platforms like Amper Music and Runway allow artists to produce unique visuals and sounds, enriching the listener's experience beyond just the music.

Synthesized Sounds - A New Era

16.3.3. Harness Data Analytics for Audience Insights
> ➢ AI-powered analytics platforms can analyze streaming data, social media interactions, and website traffic to provide insights into your audience's preferences and behavior. Use these insights to refine your music style, content, and engagement strategies.

Example: Spotify for Artists provides detailed insights into who listens to your music, helping you identify potential new markets.

16.3.4. Engage with Fans Using Chatbots and AI Assistants
> ➢ AI chatbots allow for real-time fan interaction, creating a personalized experience for your audience. These bots can answer questions, share updates, and even recommend music based on user input.

Example: Deploy a chatbot on your website or social media to handle merchandise queries or promote upcoming releases, fostering a sense of connection with your fans.

16.3.5. Build a Strong Social Media Presence
> ➢ AI can help you create captivating social media content by analyzing trending topics and recommending hashtags. Additionally, AI-generated content such as teaser videos or music previews can keep your audience engaged.

Example: Tools like Canva or Lumen5 can assist in creating professional-grade visuals and videos for your music promotion.

16.3.6. Collaborate with AI Creators and Influencers

➤ Collaborations with AI musicians or influencers who use AI tools can amplify your reach. Partnering with AI-powered creators not only expands your audience but also showcases your adaptability in the tech-driven music world.

Example: Collaborate with AI influencers on TikTok or Instagram to create viral challenges featuring your music.

16.3.7. Personalize the Listening Experience

➤ AI can create personalized listening experiences by curating playlists or remixing tracks based on individual listener preferences. Offering customized music to fans enhances their loyalty and engagement.

Example: Use platforms like Endel to create personalized soundscapes for your listeners.

16.3.8. Diversify Revenue Streams with AI Integration

➤ AI tools can help you diversify your income through new monetization avenues. Consider licensing your music for AI-generated content, offering subscription-based experiences, or selling AI-generated merchandise.

Example: Platforms like Patreon allow you to offer exclusive AI-enhanced content to your most dedicated fans.

17- Maintaining Artistic Integrity in AI Collaboration

17.1 Navigating the Challenges of Authenticity in an AI-Driven World

In an era where artificial intelligence has become an integral tool in the music industry, maintaining authenticity is a complex yet vital endeavor. As artists collaborate with AI to create music, the fine line between innovation and imitation is often blurred. The challenge lies in ensuring that the resulting work remains true to the artist's identity, while leveraging AI's potential to amplify creativity.

17.1.1

Authenticity in music has historically been rooted in human emotion, personal experiences, and cultural contexts. However, when AI generates melodies, lyrics, or even entire compositions, questions arise about the source of artistic expression. Can a machine truly embody the soul of an artist, or does it merely mimic patterns learned from vast datasets? These questions compel creators to reflect on their role in shaping the narrative of their music.

17.1.2

To navigate these challenges, artists must consciously define their boundaries with AI. It requires striking a balance between delegating technical tasks to AI—like mixing or mastering—and retaining human oversight in areas where emotional depth and personal touch are paramount. Transparency is equally important; sharing the role of AI in the creative process can foster trust and appreciation among audiences.

17.1.3

Moreover, understanding the capabilities and limitations of AI is crucial. While AI can analyze trends and predict audience preferences, over-reliance risks diluting originality. Artists should view AI as a collaborator, not a replacement, ensuring their vision and intent remain the driving force behind every composition.

The journey of maintaining artistic integrity in an AI-driven world is a testament to the resilience and adaptability of creators. By embracing AI as a tool rather than a threat, artists can forge a new path where technology enhances, rather than eclipses, the essence of human creativity.

17.2 Strategies for Blending Human and AI Creativity

As the symphony of human creativity and AI technology grows louder, a harmonious blend of the two is essential to ensure artistic integrity. AI offers unprecedented opportunities to innovate in music creation, but without strategic collaboration, it risks overshadowing the human essence that forms the heart of art. Here are key strategies for blending human and AI creativity while preserving authenticity:

17.2.1. Leverage AI as a Tool, Not a Replacement
> ➢ AI should enhance your creative process, not replace it. Treat AI as a collaborator that can handle technical

or repetitive tasks, like generating harmonic layers or suggesting melodic variations, allowing you to focus on the emotive and thematic aspects of your work.

17.2.2. Define Creative Boundaries

➢ Establish clear guidelines for the role AI plays in your projects. Will it act as an assistant, a co-composer, or merely an analytical tool? By defining its scope, you ensure that your artistic vision remains at the forefront while utilizing AI's strengths.

17.2.3. Emphasize Human-Led Decision Making

➢ While AI can provide suggestions, the final decisions should always rest with the artist. Infuse your personal style and emotional intent into the project, ensuring the music resonates with a human audience on a deeper level.

17.2.4. Co-create Through Iterative Feedback

➢ Use AI as a partner in a dynamic, iterative process. Generate initial compositions using AI, refine them with your input, and continue this loop until the piece aligns with your vision. This ensures a seamless integration of AI's efficiency and your creativity.

17.2.5. Incorporate Emotional Context

➢ AI lacks the inherent emotional depth and life experiences of a human creator. Bridge this gap by embedding personal stories, cultural influences, and emotional nuances into your work, ensuring that the final output reflects a uniquely human touch.

17.2.6. Explore AI-Driven Innovation While Honoring Tradition

➢ AI offers tools for pushing creative boundaries, like generating novel soundscapes or experimenting with unconventional structures. However, balance this with respect for musical traditions, ensuring your work remains both innovative and grounded.

17.2.7. Foster Transparency in Collaboration

➢ Be open about the role AI played in your creative process. This transparency not only builds trust with your audience but also sparks meaningful conversations about the evolving role of technology in music.

17.2.8. Engage in Continuous Learning

➢ Stay updated on the latest AI advancements and how they can be integrated into your craft. Equally, deepen your knowledge of musical theory and history to maintain a strong human foundation in your work.

17.2.9. Promote Ethical Use of AI

➢ Ensure that your AI tools respect copyright laws and ethical standards. Avoid over-reliance on AI-generated works that could infringe on existing artistry, safeguarding the integrity of the creative community.

17.2.10. Celebrate the Unpredictable

➢ One of the strengths of AI is its ability to surprise with unexpected outputs. Embrace these moments of serendipity as opportunities for new directions, allowing AI to expand your creative horizons without compromising your artistic identity.

Synthesized Sounds - A New Era

In this era of synthesized sounds, the key to maintaining artistic integrity lies in recognizing that creativity thrives in collaboration, not competition. By strategically blending the best of human intuition with AI's computational power, artists can usher in a new era of music that resonates deeply, innovates boldly, and stays true to its artistic core.

17.3 Understanding the Perceptions of Audiences Towards AI-Created Music

In the rapidly evolving landscape of AI-driven creativity, understanding how audiences perceive AI-created music is pivotal to maintaining artistic integrity. As technology and artistry intertwine, listeners often grapple with questions about authenticity, emotional resonance, and creative ownership.

17.3.1

These perceptions directly influence the acceptance and success of AI-generated compositions in the music industry.

A critical aspect of audience perception lies in the emotional depth of AI-created music. Many listeners associate music with profound human experiences and may question whether AI can truly replicate or evoke such emotional intricacies. Skepticism often stems from the idea that AI, devoid of lived experiences, may lack the capacity for genuine artistic expression. However, this viewpoint is evolving as AI systems increasingly integrate human input, such as data from emotional patterns or collaborative frameworks with artists, to craft music that resonates deeply.

17.3.2

Transparency in the creative process is another vital factor shaping audience perceptions. When musicians openly acknowledge the role of AI in their compositions, it fosters trust and curiosity rather than resistance. Audiences are more likely to appreciate AI as a tool that enhances creativity rather than diminishes the artist's role. This openness transforms the narrative from one of replacement to collaboration, preserving the authenticity of the musical experience.

17.3.3

Moreover, generational and cultural differences significantly impact how AI-generated music is received. Younger, tech-savvy audiences may embrace such music as a natural progression of innovation, while traditionalists might view it as a departure from human-centered artistry. Understanding these varied perspectives enables creators to tailor their approach, ensuring that the integrity of their work resonates across diverse demographics.

Ultimately, the challenge for artists working with AI is to balance technological innovation with emotional authenticity. By addressing audience concerns and embracing collaboration, AI musicians can bridge the gap between art and technology, reinforcing the idea that creativity thrives not despite AI but because of it. This nuanced understanding is essential for shaping a future where AI-generated music is celebrated as a legitimate and emotionally compelling art form.

18- The Global Impact of AI on Music Culture

18.1 How AI is Influencing Diverse Musical Genres Worldwide

Artificial Intelligence (AI) has become a transformative force across various musical genres, reshaping the creative and production processes globally. From classical compositions to experimental electronic beats, AI tools are enabling artists to push the boundaries of music, explore cross-genre innovations, and reach audiences in unprecedented ways.

18.1.1

AI-powered algorithms analyze vast datasets of existing music to understand stylistic patterns and emotional undertones specific to genres. For instance, in jazz, AI tools like OpenAI's MuseNet can improvise harmonies and melodies that mimic the fluidity of a live jazz performance. Similarly, in electronic dance music (EDM), AI-based synthesizers are helping producers create unique sounds by blending human creativity with machine precision.

18.1.2

The impact of AI extends beyond creation into the realm of collaboration. Musicians in culturally diverse regions are integrating AI to fuse traditional sounds with modern genres. For example, African beats have been reimagined using AI tools to combine tribal rhythms with contemporary hip-hop. Likewise, in Indian classical music, AI is assisting in crafting raga-based compositions that appeal to global audiences while maintaining their authenticity.

18.1.3
Additionally, AI-driven recommendation engines are reshaping how music is discovered, ensuring that niche genres such as folk, indie, or experimental music find their way to listeners worldwide. Streaming platforms leverage AI to curate personalized playlists that introduce audiences to diverse styles, fostering cross-cultural appreciation and influence.

18.1.4
AI's influence is not limited to established genres but also contributes to the birth of entirely new musical styles. By generating non-human melodies, rhythms, and harmonies, AI encourages artists to experiment with sounds that may not naturally occur, giving rise to innovative subgenres.

In this era of "Synthesized Sounds," AI is not replacing human artistry but amplifying its scope. By breaking geographical and creative barriers, it's ensuring that music continues to evolve as a universal language of expression.

18.2 Cross-Cultural Collaborations Facilitated by AI Technology

In the ever-evolving landscape of music, Artificial Intelligence (AI) has proven to be a powerful tool that transcends geographical, linguistic, and cultural boundaries. Through AI technology, musicians and producers from different corners of the world can collaborate seamlessly, sharing their unique musical identities and creating innovative fusion genres that blend diverse cultural elements. AI's ability to analyze, learn, and generate music patterns has enabled musicians to experiment with sounds from various cultural backgrounds, leading to the creation of entirely new musical genres.

18.2.1

AI-driven music platforms and tools offer unprecedented opportunities for cross-cultural exchanges. Music professionals can now access vast databases of global music styles and sounds, using AI to mix, enhance, and transform these elements into fresh compositions. Whether it's integrating African rhythms with Western electronic beats or blending traditional Indian instruments with contemporary pop melodies, AI serves as a bridge that connects musicians from different cultural backgrounds in real-time.

18.2.2

Additionally, AI-powered music software and applications are breaking down language barriers by creating music that resonates with audiences across cultures. Natural Language Processing (NLP) and sentiment analysis tools are capable of interpreting emotions and nuances in lyrics, allowing musicians to adapt their messages to appeal to diverse audiences worldwide. AI's ability to quickly translate and adapt musical ideas has made it easier for artists to collaborate on a global scale, creating music that celebrates both universal themes and regional influences.

In essence, AI is fostering a new era of music that is inclusive, diverse, and open to experimentation. Through cross-cultural collaborations, musicians are able to explore new sonic landscapes and amplify their creative

Synthesized Sounds - A New Era

potential. For aspiring artists looking to build a career in AI-driven music, the ability to collaborate across cultures is no longer a distant dream but a tangible reality, one that allows them to showcase their talents on a global stage while celebrating the richness of musical traditions worldwide.

18.3 Exploring Global Trends and Challenges in AI Music

The emergence of artificial intelligence (AI) in the music industry is nothing short of revolutionary, shaping how music is created, consumed, and experienced across the globe. As AI continues to evolve, it influences a broad spectrum of trends and challenges, offering both opportunities and concerns for musicians, producers, and audiences alike.

18.3.1

One of the most significant trends is the increasing use of AI to compose and produce music. AI-driven tools are now capable of generating melodies, harmonies, and entire compositions based on a set of input parameters, from simple motifs to complex genres. These tools have lowered the barrier to entry for aspiring musicians, enabling those without traditional training to explore their creative potential. However, the accessibility of such tools raises questions about authorship, originality, and the definition of "art" itself. If a machine can create music indistinguishable from human compositions, what role does the artist play?

18.3.2

Moreover, AI is revolutionizing the personalization of music consumption. Platforms like Spotify and Apple Music utilize AI algorithms to curate playlists and recommend songs, tailoring the listening experience to individual tastes and preferences. While this personalization enhances user experience, it also creates a homogenous ecosystem that might limit exposure to diverse genres, regions, and artists. This trend highlights the potential of AI to both democratize music discovery and restrict the breadth of musical diversity.

18.3.3

On the production side, AI tools have enhanced music production efficiency, enabling the automation of tedious tasks such as mastering, mixing, and sound design. For instance, AI software can analyze a song's structure and suggest edits or improvements, often with a speed and precision that outpaces human capabilities. This has led to the rise of "AI producers," who use algorithms to shape tracks in innovative ways. While this development could lead to a new wave of production styles, it has also spurred concerns about the loss of human touch and emotional depth in music creation.

18.3.4

However, as AI integrates deeper into the music landscape, it introduces complex challenges. One key issue is the ethical dilemma surrounding intellectual property rights. With AI-created music, determining ownership becomes a gray area. Who owns the rights to a song composed by an algorithm: the developer of the AI, the user who provided the input, or the AI itself? Legal frameworks are struggling to keep up with these questions, leading to uncertainty for musicians and technology developers alike.

Synthesized Sounds - A New Era

18.3.5

Additionally, there is a growing concern about the displacement of human musicians. While AI can assist in the creation of music, there are fears that it could eventually replace human creativity entirely, especially in commercial contexts where cost-effectiveness and productivity are prioritized. The risk of reduced job opportunities for musicians and other industry professionals is a pressing challenge that requires careful consideration as the technology develops.

18.3.6

Lastly, global trends in AI music also highlight disparities in access to technology. In regions with limited resources or technological infrastructure, musicians may be at a disadvantage, unable to benefit from AI tools that could enhance their careers. As AI becomes increasingly vital in shaping the future of music, it is crucial to ensure that its benefits are equitably distributed, preventing a digital divide that leaves certain voices unheard.

Exploring global trends and challenges in AI music presents a dynamic landscape where innovation and disruption coexist. As the industry continues to embrace AI, it is vital for stakeholders—musicians, technologists, policymakers, and consumers—to navigate the ethical, social, and economic implications, ensuring that AI contributes to a more inclusive, diverse, and human-centric music culture.

19- Your Path to an AI-Driven Music Career

19.1 Actionable Steps for Starting a Career in AI Music

Embarking on a career in AI music combines technical expertise, creativity, and a passion for innovation. By following these steps, you can carve your path in this dynamic field:

19.1.1. Build a Strong Foundation in Music and Technology

- ➢ **Learn Music Theory**: Familiarize yourself with the basics of music composition, scales, chords, and rhythm.
- ➢ **Understand Sound Design**: Explore digital audio workstations (DAWs) like Ableton Live, Logic Pro, or FL Studio to experiment with music creation.
- ➢ **Study Programming Basics**: Acquire skills in programming languages like Python, which are essential for working with AI algorithms and machine learning frameworks.

19.1.2. Master Key Tools and Technologies

- ➢ **AI and Machine Learning Frameworks**: Learn TensorFlow, PyTorch, or similar platforms to develop AI models for music generation.
- ➢ **Audio Processing Tools**: Explore libraries like Librosa, Essentia, or Sonic Visualizer for analyzing and processing audio data.
- ➢ **Music AI Platforms**: Experiment with tools like OpenAI's MuseNet, AIVA, or Amper Music to understand how AI is used in composing music.

19.1.3. Develop a Portfolio
- ➢ **Showcase Your Work**: Create and publish AI-generated music pieces on platforms like SoundCloud or YouTube.
- ➢ **Participate in Collaborations**: Work with musicians, producers, or other AI enthusiasts to create innovative projects.
- ➢ **Build Case Studies**: Document the technical and creative processes behind your projects to demonstrate your expertise.

19.1.4. Stay Updated on Industry Trends
- ➢ **Follow AI Music Innovations**: Stay informed about new algorithms, tools, and breakthroughs in AI music by subscribing to blogs, journals, and newsletters.
- ➢ **Engage with Communities**: Join online forums like AI Music forums, Reddit groups, or Discord channels where professionals and enthusiasts share knowledge.

19.1.5. Enhance Your Skills Through Courses and Certifications
- ➢ **Pursue Formal Education**: Consider enrolling in courses that specialize in AI, music production, or a combination of both. Platforms like Coursera, edX, or Udemy offer specialized programs.
- ➢ **Earn Certifications**: Obtain recognized certifications in machine learning, music production, or AI development to bolster your credentials.

19.1.6. Network with Professionals in the Field
- ➢ **Attend Events**: Participate in AI music conferences, hackathons, and expos to connect with industry leaders and innovators.

Synthesized Sounds - A New Era

➢ **Seek Mentorship**: Find mentors in AI music who can guide your career and provide valuable insights.

19.1.7. Explore Career Opportunities

➢ **Join Startups or Research Labs**: Look for roles in organizations focusing on AI music technology development.

➢ **Freelance Projects**: Offer your skills for bespoke AI music projects, including jingles, background scores, or experimental compositions.

➢ **Create Your Own Venture**: Consider launching your startup in AI-driven music solutions, such as generative composition or interactive soundscapes.

19.1.8. Experiment and Innovate

➢ **Push Creative Boundaries**: Combine AI tools with your unique style to create music that resonates with audiences.

➢ **Test Novel Ideas**: Experiment with integrating AI in performance art, live shows, or immersive installations.

➢ By taking these actionable steps, you'll position yourself at the forefront of the AI music revolution, ready to contribute to and thrive in this exciting fusion of tunes and tech.

Synthesized Sounds - A New Era

19.2 Building a Personal Portfolio and Showcasing Your Work

In the evolving world of AI-driven music, your portfolio is more than a collection of projects; it's your identity as a creator. A well-crafted portfolio not only showcases your technical proficiency but also highlights your artistic vision and ability to merge creativity with technology.

19.2.1 The Importance of a Personal Portfolio

An effective portfolio serves as a bridge between you and potential collaborators, employers, or clients. It demonstrates your ability to harness AI tools and techniques to compose, produce, and innovate in music. In a field where technology evolves rapidly, a dynamic portfolio reflects your commitment to growth and staying current with industry trends.

19.2.2 What to Include in Your Portfolio
19.2.2.1 Original AI-Generated Compositions:

➢ Share pieces that demonstrate your understanding of AI tools and their creative applications. Highlight how you used AI to compose melodies, harmonize, or create experimental soundscapes.

19.2.2.2 Collaborative Projects:

➢ If you've worked with other artists or technologists, showcase projects that emphasize teamwork and interdisciplinary skills.

19.2.2.3 Before-and-After Tracks:
➢ Include examples showing how AI enhanced or transformed traditional music pieces. This highlights your problem-solving skills and the tangible impact of AI.

19.2.2.4 Case Studies or Explanations:
➢ Briefly describe the creative and technical processes behind your works. For instance, discuss how you trained a neural network to emulate a specific genre or how AI-assisted mixing tools improved production quality.

19.2.2.5 Testimonials:
➢ Include feedback from collaborators or listeners to add credibility and context to your achievements.

19.2.3 Platforms to Showcase Your Work
➢ In today's digital-first environment, accessibility matters. Host your portfolio on platforms that cater to diverse audiences:

19.2.3.1 Personal Website:
➢ Create a dedicated site with sections for your music, project descriptions, and a blog discussing AI and music trends.

19.2.3.2 SoundCloud or Bandcamp:
➢ Share audio tracks to reach a global audience of music enthusiasts.

19.2.3.3 GitHub or GitLab:
➢ If your work includes open-source code or technical insights, these platforms are ideal for showcasing your programming expertise.

19.2.3.4 Social Media and Networking Sites:
➢ Share snippets, updates, and behind-the-scenes glimpses on platforms like Instagram, LinkedIn, or TikTok to engage with varied audiences.

19.2.4 Staying Authentic
Your portfolio should reflect your unique style and goals. Whether you aim to compose symphonies with AI, develop tools for music production, or bridge cultural gaps through synthesized sounds, your portfolio is the story of your journey. Be authentic, as it will resonate with audiences who value originality and passion.

Building a personal portfolio isn't just a step in your career, it's an ongoing process that evolves with your skills, experiences, and aspirations. With the right approach, it becomes your most powerful tool in the AI-driven music industry, opening doors to opportunities and collaborations in this exciting new era.

19.3 Inspirational Closing Thoughts and Encouragement for Aspiring Musicians

As we conclude this chapter, let's pause to celebrate the incredible journey you are embarking on in the realm of AI-driven music. The fusion of tunes and tech has unlocked boundless possibilities, making this an exhilarating time to be a creator. The tools at your

disposal are more powerful than ever, but it's your unique vision and creativity that will shape the future of music.

Remember, every great musician started somewhere often with just a dream and the courage to pursue it. The same holds true for you. Embracing AI doesn't mean replacing your artistry; it means enhancing it, pushing the boundaries of what you thought possible. The melody of innovation is calling, and it's up to you to answer with passion and perseverance.

Failures and challenges are part of the process, but so are breakthroughs and moments of pure magic. Stay curious, keep experimenting, and don't shy away from collaboration whether with fellow humans or intelligent algorithms. Your path will be uniquely yours, carved by the rhythm of your ambitions and the beats of your determination.

The future of music is waiting for pioneers like you to define it. Let your voice and vision shine, not just through your compositions but through the legacy of creativity you leave behind. This is your era—an era of synthesized sounds and limitless potential.

Step boldly into this new world, and let the music of tomorrow flow through you. The stage is yours. Play it loud, play it proud, and most importantly, play it true to your heart.

Synthesized Sounds - A New Era

Conclusion

As we journey through Synthesized Sounds: A New Era, it becomes evident that the intersection of music and artificial intelligence is not just a fleeting trend but a transformative force reshaping the way we create, experience, and share music. From exploring the roots of synthesized sounds to understanding the tools and techniques for building a career in AI-driven music production, this book aims to serve as a roadmap for aspiring creators and innovators.

Through the lens of technology and creativity, the possibilities for artists, engineers, and enthusiasts are limitless. The integration of AI in music not only offers new methods of composition and performance but also invites a reimagining of traditional career pathways in the industry.

Deepak Kumar Mahanta, with his rich academic background in electronics, video communication engineering, and business administration, has woven together his expertise to present a holistic perspective. His vision is to inspire readers to embrace the opportunities of this new era while maintaining the core essence of artistic expression.

As you step into this evolving landscape, may the lessons and insights from this book empower you to innovate, collaborate, and contribute meaningfully to the future of music. Let the harmony of technology and creativity guide your path as you compose the soundtrack of a new era.

www.ingramcontent.com/pod-product-compliance
Lightning Source LLC
LaVergne TN
LVHW041213050326
832903LV00021B/598